My Shot

THE VERY BEST INTERVIEWS FROM
Golf Digest MAGAZINE

GUY YOCOM

Stewart, Tabori & Chang New York

Published in 2007 by Stewart, Tabori & Chang
An imprint of Harry N. Abrams, Inc.

Copyright © 2007 by Golf Digest Publications

Library of Congress Cataloging-in-Publication Data
Yocom, Guy.
   My shot : the very best interviews from Golf digest
magazine / Guy Yocom.
     p. cm.
  ISBN-13: 978-1-58479-637-4
  ISBN-10: 1-58479-637-5
  1. Golfers—Interviews. I. Golf digest. II. Title.
GV964.A1Y63 2007
796.3520922—dc22
  [B]   2007011264

Editor: Jennifer Levesque
Designer: Laura Lindgren
Production Manager: Jacquie Poirier
Photo Editor: Matthew Ginella

The text of this book was composed in Garth Graphic and Avenir.

Printed and bound in China
10 9 8 7 6 5 4 3 2 1
First printing

HNA

harry n. abrams, inc.

a subsidiary of La Martinière Groupe

115 West 18th Street
New York, NY 10011
www.hnabooks.com

Contents

Introduction

It's hard to say when it became clear that the *My Shot* series in *Golf Digest* should be made available in one place. It may have been shortly after Sam Snead explained how he caught a bobcat with his bare hands, or when Doug Sanders told the harrowing story of ordering his own murder. It may have been when Moe Norman, the world's best ball striker, revealed how he was once relegated to sleeping on park benches, which was why he carried $10,000 in cash in his front pocket at all times.

So many interesting revelations came forth in the series—hundreds of them, as you'll see—that at some point it seemed natural to turn them into a book. In any case, the result, which you are holding, is a compilation of extraordinary people talking about golf, life, and most important, themselves.

Evel Knievel tells of wild golf gambling games, going to jail, and finagling a way to play golf from "the yard."... Samuel L. Jackson discloses that he brought his *Star Wars* light saber from the set and pulled it from his golf bag during waits on the par 3s to practice his strokes.... Jack Nicklaus grows misty reliving a funeral attended by Woody Hayes.... Laura Baugh tells about the depths of her alcoholism in a way that will make anybody's hair stand on end.... Lee Trevino speculates that he will be reincarnated as an eagle.... JoAnne Carner explains how her bosom robbed her of distance with the driver. These are random examples of the things golfers talk about away from the stage, in the company of friends. They are what make the *My Shot* series, and this book, special.

There is wisdom and advice on living a fruitful life. Jackie Burke tells us to "Live your life so that when you die, you fill up the church." Sam Snead suggests we buy real estate. Greg Norman advises that you never be the guarantor on an investment. The late Earl Woods offers tips on child rearing, while double-amputee Bob Wilson explains the keys to recovering from personal disaster. There also is much practical advice on playing the game: Billy Casper on putting, Jack Nicklaus on tempo, and Gary Player on the curious nature of slumps. Tom Watson expounds on how to beat the yips, Byron Nelson explains how hard you should swing, and Tommy Bolt says, "Never break your driver and putter in the same round." Yes, there is humor, too.

The *My Shot* feature was inspired by *Esquire* magazine's excellent *What I've Learned* series. The editors at *Golf Digest* had been looking for an alternative to the standard question-and-answer format, and the *Esquire* piece was very well done. We originally conceived the *My Shot* to be a one- or two-off thing, a means to profile a legendary player in the first-person voice. I quickly chose as my subject the great Slammin'

Sam, whom I'd gotten to know fairly well over the years. There seemed to be no end to the golf stories Sam had told me, and I hoped to have him give me two thousand or so good words that could be distilled to eight hundred great ones. Sam granted me a visit, and following an important logistical assist from his son Jack, I spent two days with Sam in and around his home in Hot Springs, Virginia.

Sam was fabulous, and as I typed up my notes I was not at all put off by the fact that he'd kept directing the conversations away from golf. In the draft I submitted, Sam told us how to train a bass and how to befriend a deer. He spouted his peculiar thoughts on religion and the afterlife, reminisced on his stint in the Navy during World War II, and offered his blunt opinion on how to handle terrorists post–9/11. He issued mea culpas on endorsing cigarettes that he didn't smoke, and confessed to a character flaw he felt mitigated his basic charitable good-

ness. He talked of his father's prowess at checkers and told of the four-string banjo he got at Christmas as a boy. There was his affinity for haircuts and back rubs, sirloin steaks cooked medium, and the satisfaction he derived from mending his own shirts. He gossiped, complained, laughed, bragged a little, yelled, and got tears in his eyes at least twice.

Who could resist this stuff? All 2,500 words were keepers. They took the full measure of Slammin' Sam. His focusing on the peripheral aspects of his life was rare for him—and for *Golf Digest*. The story as a whole emitted a sense of urgency, as though Sam were aiming for posterity. Looking back, I think Sam at age eighty-nine felt his time was short. He wanted to outline his legacy not just as a great champion, but as a man.

After photographer Ben Van Hook delivered one of the more powerful portraits of Sam ever taken—a pensive Slammer looking askance at the viewfinder, his trademark hat gone for once—the editors quite predictably asked, "Who do you have for next month?"

Eventually the *My Shot* series stretched to more than five years and sixty-plus installments. Sam passed away a few months after our visit, but five years down the road, I'm very thankful to him for helping turn the standard Q&A interview treatment on its ear and setting a standard for the subjects who followed. Very rarely have I failed to send a prospective interview subject that first *My Shot* with Sam, explaining what I'd be shooting for when we got together. It made many of them gulp.

Early on, I formulated a couple of ground rules that made the interviews more productive. One is the "cocktail party directive," based on the old bit of social advice suggesting that, if you find yourself at a social and know precious few people there, immediately seek out either a priest or the oldest person in the room. In short, I sought out people who were old enough to have gotten the full treatment out of their life and careers. With the exception of the delightful Michelle Wie, who was fourteen when I met up with her in Orlando, Florida, none of the people I've interviewed are under the age of forty-five. In searching for wisdom, advice, reflections on the past, and speculations on the future, you want subjects who have accumulated years and plenty of mileage. Moreover, older people are not only more inclined to talk, they are better at it—they were around in the days when they had to promote the game, not just play it. With due respect to tour pros under the age of thirty, they tend to give

pleasure primarily with their golf clubs. How many have provided memorable TV and magazine interviews? They rarely peel back more than a half-layer of skin. The older guys have always sensed what I was looking for and delivered, because they are unafraid of the truth.

It also helps that *My Shot* is collaborative. I always assured the individuals that they could review the piece and revise it if they felt they spoke too indelicately about a topic. I feared that taking this step would result in items being crossed out en masse, but in fact it very rarely happened. Most of them never altered a word, and I doubt that more than two dozen paragraphs out of thousands were deleted. When a story told by the subject approached the line—Sanders and his

planned suicide is the best example—I was able to persuade them that the item belonged in the context of their whole life experience. People I expected to be cautious, such as Arnold Palmer and Jack Nicklaus, turned out to be expansive and forthright.

The other rules were a luxury of *Golf Digest* being a prominent magazine. I requested at least two hours in a quiet place with the subject and was granted that in all but the case of Greg Norman, whose schedule is so busy that I was lucky to obtain an hour on the distant island of Anguilla, east of Puerto Rico. Billy Casper gave me a full day at his home in Utah. Jack Nicklaus gave me more than two hours on his private plane. I traveled, incidentally, to more than fifty cities and fifteen states to acquire the *My Shots*. I suppose it's not surprising that I caught up with five subjects in Orlando.

Ultimately the interviews bore more fruit than we imagined they would. I would sometimes turn in upward of seven thousand words, when two pages of text in *Golf Digest* could accommodate only eighteen hundred words. The solution was to jump the interviews beyond the main editorial well. Even then it was unfortunate to see pretty nice passages land on the cutting-room floor. But that's baseball.

I've mentioned Ben Van Hook's fantastic portrait of Sam, and as you'll see the accompanying photographs of every subject are almost as vital as the text itself. Some of the shots had our editors wringing their hands with excitement—no small feat. My favorite is of Tom Weiskopf, who told a wonderful story of his childhood fascination with the Lone Ranger. It turned out that Weiskopf owns horses, one of whom bears a resemblance to the Lone Ranger's steed, Silver. Chip Simons rooted out a Lone Ranger costume, and a game Weiskopf posed for the most remarkable photograph

in the series. Others were about as good. Billy Casper loved the first nickname he acquired on tour, "the Gorilla." He not only donned the gorilla suit, but proffered a fierce, gorillalike snarl. Long-driving king Sean (the Beast) Fister posed as a circus strongman. Course architect Pete Dye stood with a simple pushmower. Gary Player posed shirtless, showcasing his considerable physique. Lee Trevino posed with an eagle borrowed from a zoo in Dallas. The pugnacious Jackie Burke stood next to a bulldog.

For three of the subjects, the portraits turned out to be among the last ever taken. Earl Woods and Byron Nelson passed away in 2006. Moe Norman died less than a month after I interviewed him in 2005. I'll miss them. They were so generous in giving me far more than a glimpse into the traits that made them special.

—Guy Yocom

Sam Snead

A year before I visited Sam for the introductory *My Shot* in 2002, I traveled with him and his son Jack from his winter home in Fort Pierce, Florida, to Augusta, Georgia, for the Masters. Sam suffered something resembling a stroke en route and was admitted to the hospital in Augusta upon his arrival. He was released in time to take part in the Honorary Starter ceremony, and as I was with him virtually the whole time, we became friends. My visit to his home in Virginia, where we did the interview, was lengthy and enjoyable, and Sam was never more relaxed. I gained much insight into the man many considered the best natural golfer who ever lived.

Sam died a few months after the interview, but he was sharp to the end. As he dropped me off at my hotel and bade me good-bye, he told me not to hold the club so tightly with my right hand. "What?" I stammered. I hadn't picked up a club during my visit. "I can tell by the way you hold that pen that your grip is too tight," he said.

o o o

You can't catch a fish unless you keep your line in the water. You have to be patient. A cold wind can be blowing and ice can be forming on your eyebrows, but you have to keep at it.

When I was in training for tournaments, I went to bed at eight every night and got up at sunrise. But I never slept ten hours straight. It seemed I would wake up for three hours during the night and just lay there and think about golf.

I've still got the four-string Gibson banjo I ordered from a Sears catalog when I was fourteen. It took me three years to save enough money to buy it. It may be the most precious thing I own. Nobody has played it but me.

Some people aren't cut out to play golf—mentally, physically, or both. You've seen the people I'm talking about. It comes to a point where they should just find a different hobby.

My favorite meal has always been a sirloin steak cooked medium, a baked potato with nothing on it, and a green salad with two tablespoons of oil and vinegar dressing. For fifty years I avoided dessert, but now I eat all the ice cream I want.

A lot of old people come to accept the thought of dying. Not me. Dying scares the hell out of me. I want to live forever.

I didn't touch a drop of liquor until I was in my sixties. I never saw the point in starting. When I was young I saw drinking ruin a lot of golfers and celebrities. Today, though, a Diet Coke with some dark rum in it takes away some of my aches and pains.

When I was a kid, I would take my rifle and hunt my way into school each morning. Eventually I hunted all kinds of game all over the world. But one day I just stopped. I came to a point where I enjoyed feeding animals more than killing them.

Could I have whipped Tiger Woods? Hell, yes. In my prime I could do anything with a golf ball I wanted. No man scared me on the golf course.

If you can't pay cash for it, you can't afford it. Except for a house.

The sportswriters started calling me Slammin' Sam in the late 1930s. I never liked it very much. I really preferred the nickname I got when I first joined the tour: Swingin' Sam. That was the name that showed off my true strengths: smoothness and rhythm. Somehow people liked Slammin' Sam better.

The best things about being famous? I get good tables in restaurants, and the state trooper lets me go once in a while.

The best golf exercise is hiking up and down steep hills. It helps strengthen your legs, which drive your whole body. You build up your wind, too. Golfers need wind more than you think. Under pressure it's hard to breathe properly, and if you can't catch your breath, your touch will suffer. You can't concentrate, either.

Every man should learn to cook, sew, and garden. If you can do those three things, you'll always be able to take care of yourself.

I told my son Jackie that when I'm gone he should never sell the Snead farm. Because no matter how bad things get, he'll always be able to grow enough to eat.

It still drives me crazy when a man doesn't take his hat off indoors, have his shoes shined, or have clean fingernails.

A man on TV the other day said we should capture those terrorists and give them a fair trial. That made sense to me for a minute. Then I looked at some pictures of my grandchildren and thought, we should take no prisoners. Because those people want my grandchildren dead.

Never make a golf bet where you have to shoot even par (with your handicap strokes) to win. Always figure you're going to shoot three or four over par.

I've never gambled in a casino. On the other hand, I've never played a round of golf where I didn't have a bit of money riding on it. With golf it wasn't gambling, because the outcome was always under my control.

People always said I had a natural swing. They thought I wasn't a hard worker. But when I was young, I'd play and practice all day, then practice more at night by my car's headlights. My hands bled. Nobody worked harder at golf than I did.

When Ben Hogan died, I said it felt like I'd lost a brother. Some people didn't understand that, because Ben and I never socialized and rarely talked. But we were like brothers, because we both made the other guy better. A lot of blood brothers can't say that.

Putting: It's not how, but how many. My sidesaddle style wasn't pretty to look at, but I would have putted standing on my head if it would have helped.

I've had the yips off and on for the last fifty-five years. I'm convinced they come from putting on different kinds of surfaces over a long period of time. You get to the point where your mind can't figure out how hard to hit the ball.

My golden retriever, Meister, died four years ago. I cried like a baby when I had him put down. He understood me when I talked to him; for a dog he had a big vocabulary. And he loved me more than any human ever has.

I've bought carpeting and organs for churches. Sometimes I bought homes and cars for people. But it wasn't true charity, because I always expected a thank-you in return. True charity isn't like that.

The two and a half years I spent in the Navy during World War II, dead in the middle of my prime, was good for me. It helped me grow up, gave me a better view of the world. I think every single healthy American boy should go into the service for a spell.

As I get older, I like being taken care of more and more. I like getting my hair cut, my back rubbed, my finger bandaged if I get a cut. My favorite thing is pedicures.

It goes without saying that my biggest disappointment was never winning the U.S. Open. I'm reminded of it all the time. It hurts when people remember you for the things you didn't do, rather than for the things you did do.

People who talk really fast or dart around generally have a hard time playing golf.

Most big-time swing teachers have never been under the gun, so they don't understand how a person's swing changes under pressure. As a young player, the first thing I'd want to know is how to handle the heat.

No doubt about it, a drive that flies dead straight is the hardest shot in the book to pull off. But I tried to hit it dead straight anyway. That way, if I hooked, sliced, pushed, or pulled the ball by ten yards, it would still be in play.

I have a reputation for being tight with money, and I guess it's accurate. But I can't help it. The biggest Christmas I had as a kid was when I found fifteen cents and a pair of socks under my breakfast plate. Poverty will make you respect money.

Tiger Woods is something. But from what I see, he doesn't like putting the short ones. That makes me afraid for him. He's too young for that.

I don't understand how an autograph can be worth money. How can a famous person's signature be worth anything to anyone other than the person who asked for it?

My dad was the best checkers player in the world. He saw at least five moves ahead. I never heard of him losing, and he was a checkers player his whole life.

I detest the fact that I endorsed cigarettes years ago; I didn't even smoke. Lucky Strikes, Viceroys, Chesterfields, Granger Pipe tobacco—I endorsed them all. At The Greenbrier they had those ads on the walls as decoration. I made them take them all down.

If you want to know how good you are, go to an empty field with your 9-iron, perch up a single ball, and program yourself to hit the ball exactly 125 yards. Hit the shot, then pace off the yardage. If you came within five yards, you're a player.

I could have been a better father when my kids were young. But I was gone so damned much of the time. It's never too late, though. Jackie and I see each other every day, Terry is nearby, and I can't imagine father and sons being closer than we are now.

Terry is handicapped mentally. He caught a bad fever when he was two, and he didn't

develop normally after that. But having a handicapped child has taught me to look at what they might be capable of, instead of dwelling on their limitations.

Mean dogs and ornery cats are nice to me. I've walked right up to deer and even a bobcat. I trained a bass to let me lift him out of the water. It's just a gift I have. All I do is look at them softly and move in a slow, kind way.

I can't play golf anymore. My legs won't let me walk even nine holes. But I know I'll be able to play again in the spring, after I ride my bicycle through that Bermuda grass they have around my winter home in Florida.

Michelle Wie

When Michelle Wie was fourteen years old, watching her play golf and speaking with her at length was the most incongruous experience I'd had in my career. In the spring of 2004, her swing was already powerful, sleek, elegant, and decidedly adultlike. But her physical ability was clearly—and charmingly—outrunning the little girl within. Though she had some advanced thoughts on the golf gods, karma, global warming, and forged autographs, she also turned out to be predictably self-conscious about her height (six feet), shoe size (men's nine and a half), and sitting in the front of her junior high classroom in Hawaii. Michelle was delightful, and though her parents, father B.J. and mother Bo, were present, she took some playful swipes at them. They did not interfere. Her greatest exploits are still years down the road, but we got one of the first glimpses of her developing sensibilities. It was impossible not to like her then, and though there is supposed to be no cheering in the press box, I can't help but root for her still.

o o o

Modern comedies aren't as good as the ones they used to make. I'm old school. I love *Dumb & Dumber*.

I learned most of the letters of the alphabet before I turned one and learned to read before I turned two. My parents are so proud of that. My very first memory is going down by the pool in the apartment where we lived and reading the sign that said WARNING: DON'T DIVE. I didn't know what it meant, but I could read it and knew it had something to do with danger.

Place your palms together in front of your face, like you're praying. At the same time, put your forearms together so the inside points of your elbows are touching each other. Now stretch your arms straight out, keeping your palms together. See how my elbows are still touching and yours aren't? Only a girl can do that.

I wear a size nine-and-a-half shoe. OK, so it's the men's size. But it's still only nine and a half.

Throwing clubs or getting angry is bad for your karma. In a tournament once I chunked a chip in front of a lot of people. After I finished the hole I stomped toward the next tee. There was a gallery rope there, and I tripped on it and cut my leg. I still have the scar. It was the golf gods getting even with me.

If you expect a bad lie even for one second, the gods will know it and give you a bad lie, because you deserve it for thinking that way.

My mom gets this concoction from a special Korean food store in Los Angeles. They kill a goat and put it in a pressure cooker until the meat falls off. Then they add some kind of snake, a little ginseng, and some herbs. They strain the juice and put it in a pouch, and you're supposed to drink it. It's like vomit mixed with coffee, totally disgusting, but it really increases my strength and stamina. I complain, but as my mom points out, I drink the whole thing twice a day.

Kids tend to copy their heroes. I use an interlocking grip because a long time ago, when I started playing golf, the best player in the world had an interlocking grip. I'm talking about Tiger Woods.

Jim Caviezel's initials are J.C., the same as Jesus Christ. Isn't that amazing? And did you know he was struck by lightning while he was making *The Passion of the Christ?* Sometimes I wonder, is all that just coincidence?

Ernie Els is really a good teacher. He showed me the coolest shot at the Sony Open. If you're in deep rough around the green, don't chop down on the ball or try to hack it out. Don't get frustrated, the way I used to. Instead, take a sixty-degree wedge and make a long, smooth swing. Swing harder than you think you have to, and make sure you follow through. It's totally amazing—the ball will come out high and float onto the green.

In the final of the U.S. Women's Public Links last year, my opponent and I both had three-foot putts for par on the thirty-fifth hole. The match was all square, and I made my putt. Now she had to make her three-footer. What I've never told a writer before is, I wear a pendant on my neck with Mary on it. When I have an important shot to make, I sometimes hold it in my hand and say a little prayer. It always works. This time I held the pendant and said a prayer that she'd miss the putt. And she did miss, and I wound up winning. It made me wonder, though—is that the type of thing I should pray for?

I wasn't nervous at the Public Links or at the Sony Open. I used to get really nervous on the first tee, especially in big tournaments. My teeth would chatter and I'd feel cold, but my palms would sweat. Now I don't get nervous. You can tell that I'm not in a good mood when I get really quiet and walk fast.

I'm terrified of clowns. Always have been. It's called coulrophobia, and I have it bad. The fake smile, their refusal to talk, just scares me. My mom took me to see Ronald McDonald when I was small but never took me again. I screamed and cried the whole time.

I slept for sixteen hours once. Early in the week of the Sony Open I went to bed at nine p.m. and woke up at one the next day. When I can, I'll sleep more than twelve hours, and I don't feel very good if I get less than ten. The best thing about that is, there is no such thing as jet lag for me. I can sleep anywhere. Don't be offended, but I could fall asleep right now.

The perfect date would be dinner and a movie. A short dinner, and nothing fancy. My parents took me to a French restaurant once, and the chef recognized me. Instead

of the usual seven courses, we had thirteen. We were there for three and a half hours. It was a nightmare. We'd get ready to leave, and here'd come another course.

All of my teachers have been very understanding about my traveling and missing class. Except for one. In sixth grade, one teacher left a long message on our answering machine, telling us that if I intended to miss so many days, I belonged in public school instead of private school. Some people just don't like athletes.

Global warming is a huge problem. Al Gore talks about it all the time. Have you seen *The Day After Tomorrow*? The huge hole in the ozone layer. Something has to be done about it.

You mean the PGA Tour media guide lists a player's weight and the LPGA Tour media guide doesn't? That's awesome. I think I'm overweight.

Riding in a cart is a lot more fun than walking. But only when my dad, who is the worst cart driver in the world, lets me drive.

Men on tour should be allowed to wear shorts when the temperature is in the nineties and it's humid. Gosh, the long pants are a health hazard when it's that hot. If I were one of those guys, I'd pass out. Or pretend like I was passing out, so they'd let me wear shorts.

By the time I'm old, golfers will be shooting fifty-fours. You probably won't live to see it, but I'm sure I will.

One of the best times I've ever had was when JoAnne Carner invited me to join her for a practice round at the Dinah Shore. She is one of the most funny, honest, straightforward people I've ever met. She's so young at heart, so positive. And she hits the ball a mile. My favorite young golfer is Annika Sorenstam, but my favorite old golfer is JoAnne. I wouldn't mind getting older if I could be like her.

If I ever get bored with golf, I'm going to start over and play left-handed. I have a pretty good swing left-handed already. I don't hit the ball far, but I'm a pretty good chipper.

I had a persimmon wood once. It felt so good when I hit it. The vibration that went through my hands was wonderful. Metal woods don't have that sweet feel. You can feel the face give a little at impact and can tell the ball really springs off the clubface. The persimmon feels better, but the metal woods perform better.

My autograph is ugly, but I like it. It'll be very hard to forge.

I don't mind it when I hit a ball into the woods. I think of it as an adventure. That's when golf really gets exciting and interesting.

If you're hitting the driver great and go to the range with a big bag of balls, you'll probably leave worse off than when you got there. My instructors have said you can work flaws out of your swing by practicing, but you can also work flaws into your swing. If you're swinging well, skip the range and go to the short-game area.

My ball marker has a ladybug on it. If one lands on your putter, it's a sign you'll putt very well. They've landed on my putter many times; I seem to attract them. If you kill a ladybug, the red ones with black dots, you'll have bad luck forever.

The best thing about being six feet tall is, when I play to an elevated green, I see where the ball winds up before anybody else. That's about it. I don't want to get any taller.

The worst thing about being tall? Little things. Like I went to the movies and asked the cashier for one children's ticket. She gave me a look and said, "That will be eight dollars, please." That's the adult price. I said, "No, really, I'm a kid." She refused to believe me. And I didn't have any ID to prove it.

If I could do whatever I wanted to do this afternoon I'd go movie-hopping. You know, go to a cineplex, buy one ticket, and skip from one movie to another. That will be a challenge, tall as I am. And it's not totally honest. But if I'm paying the adult price, what the heck.

Earl Woods

I never thought the essence of Earl Woods was captured well by the writers who tried to flesh him out. He was depicted as vainglorious, stubborn, brooding, presumptuous, and, of course, proud beyond words of his son. My meeting with Earl, at his condominium at Isleworth (Tiger's old pad) in Orlando, did much to background him better and help sort out who he was, and why. I'd met Earl years earlier at a couple of college tournaments when Tiger was at Stanford, but this meeting was serious, and Earl liked to play rough. He tested me early, and I countered by provoking him; we argued about everything: race relations, baseball, Tiger's on-course swearing, Canadian versus Kentucky bourbon. It was a hell of a five-hour visit, capped off by lunch at Perkins, where he flirted with the waitress and I teased him about the bacon cheeseburger he shouldn't have been eating. My respect and admiration for him only grew, and I was grateful for the words he gave me. Earl liked the galleys I sent him, but to remind me that he was in charge, he changed exactly one word on several items, none of them of substance and all of them in the last sentence. I let him know that I knew what he was up to, and we had a good laugh. Earl died in 2006, and all I can say is, it's a shame that men like him ever have to go.

o o o

Clubs like Augusta National don't discriminate. They just don't want you. There's a difference. It's a bitch not being wanted by something or someone, which is why divorces are so difficult. But I've learned to handle rejection very well. If you love yourself enough, you won't give a damn if they want you or not.

Tiger's birthday is December 30, which meant he got presents at Christmas and another batch five days later. When he was five, he started claiming he got only half a Christmas and half a birthday. He thought we bought one batch of presents and split them. I never could convince him otherwise. He left Santa Claus out of the debate and focused on Tida and me. He did get more presents. Smart kid.

When we Green Berets were in Alaska on maneuvers for a long time, nothing tasted better than hobo coffee. We'd fill a can with water, boil it, pour in some coffee, and let it brew. When it was done, we'd throw a little snow in the can, which made the grounds instantly settle to the bottom. At that point we'd dip our cups. Then we'd pour in more water and brew the same grounds. We'd do this over and over. None of the grounds got in the cup, and we'd get ten batches of coffee from a handful of grounds.

I was in the recovery room after my heart operation, with my wife and Tiger by my side. Suddenly I was in this tunnel with a bright light at the end. It got brighter, but there was no sense of moving toward it. I felt better than I ever did my entire life. Then a voice says, "Are you all right?" and it jarred me back to this Earth. Next thing I know, the nurse—it was her voice; she'd rushed in—was jacking me full of adrenaline. My blood pressure had gone almost to zero, and I had, in fact, died for a second. It scared the hell out of Tiger. Me, all I felt was a momentary pang of regret that I was back in the hospital. That tunnel was so peaceful, just like people describe. I haven't feared death since.

At age six, Tiger signed for a wrong scorecard. It was at the Junior World in San Diego, on the par-3 Presidio Hills course. He made a par on a hole, but the scorekeeper for the group put down a birdie. Tiger signed his card and was disqualified. Afterward, making sure Tiger was standing right there, I lectured the scorekeeper. Tiger stood there scowling, like, *You tell 'em, Dad.* But the lecture was for show; I winked at the scorekeeper as I talked. I wheeled on Tiger, and in a stern tone asked, "Did you sign this?" Tiger said, "Yes." I said, "Did you check it?" Now Tiger looked nervous. "No, Daddy." I told him to never trust anyone else with your scorecard. Never. Tiger's little eyes were as big as teacups. That was the end of it. He hasn't signed a wrong scorecard since.

Tiger was four. I'd say, "Why are you hitting your ball over there, Tiger?" And he'd say, "Because there's a sand twap." "Why are you going that way?" "Because there's wawa." It was course management. To this day, it may be his greatest strength.

Tiger had a stuttering problem in the first grade. Tida and I couldn't figure out why. Even the speech therapist was stumped. Then it dawned on us: Tida talked to him in Thai, and I talked to him in English. When Tiger spoke, he talked in English. The thing was, he didn't want to listen or speak in Thai. His mind was rebelling. We stopped talking in Thai, and his stuttering ceased.

Here's how you teach a child to putt. Place a ball in their right hand and have them stand sideways, like you do at address. Ask them to swivel their head sideways and look at the hole. Ask them, "Do you see the picture?" Have them look down and back up at the target two more times, allowing them to ingrain that picture in their minds. Now say, "Toss the ball across your body to the picture." It works. It makes putting intuitive. The first time I tried it with Tiger, he tossed the ball to within six inches of the hole. When I eventually handed him a putter, he did even better. He used this technique to make the crucial putt on the third playoff hole against Ernie Els in the Presidents Cup.

When Venus Williams won Wimbledon, there was her father, standing up with a sign that read IT'S VENUS' PARTY, AND NO ONE'S INVITED. I couldn't imagine doing something like that. It would embarrass Tiger, and it would embarrass me. It infuriates me when people compare me to Richard Williams, because I don't respect him.

If you're seven-eighths Irish and one-eighth Indian, you're Irish. If you're seven-eighths Irish and one-eighth black, you're black. Why is that?

Years ago the Army sent me to Germany. My first wife came with me. A landlord took us downtown to show us an apartment. And we caused a traffic jam. I mean gridlock. People got out of their cars, pointing at us as though we were aliens. I asked the landlord what they were talking about. "They're looking for your tails," he said. "When the white soldiers came through here in World War II, they told us black people had tails." Now, you can't blame the Germans for thinking we had tails. But it bothered me that American soldiers would perpetuate such a thing.

I could quit smoking if I wanted to. I have tremendous willpower. A while back I quit for eighteen months. But then I went to my daughter's college graduation. Got stuck in my ex-wife's house with all her relatives. I snapped and lit up. Been smoking ever since.

Lying about your score or cheating at golf is really stealing. They constitute the worst kind of stealing, which is stealing from yourself. There is no end to the misery this brings on a person. I taught this to Tiger at a very young age, and to this day he's incapable of lying. He may not give you a full answer, but he never lies. The one time Tiger lied as a boy, he got physically ill.

When you get angry, you give up power. You allow outside influences to harm your greatest asset—yourself. That's why I've gotten angry at someone only twice in my life. The subject of my anger I'll keep to myself. But that person said it was very frightening.

My mother told me I was as good as anybody else, but to have an equal chance, I'd have to do better than the next person. She told me never to judge anybody, to devote myself to being proactive, positive, and constructive. That's how I've run my life, and as a result I haven't had time to feel bitter or hostile about the inequities associated with being a black man in America.

Race consciousness and prejudice will never disappear in America. It can't, because it's embedded in our language. A minute ago you referred to "little white lies." Why isn't it a "little black lie"? Why is it "blackmail" and not "whitemail"? Why do good guys wear the white hats? Invariably, the word *black* is used to refer to something derogatory, dangerous, or inferior. It creates a stigma, and so long as it exists—and I can't imagine it ever changing—there will be a separation between black and white.

I was watching a documentary about the famine in Ethiopia. Tiger, who was four, saw the distended bellies and the inability of the children to even swat flies off their faces. Tiger disappeared into his bedroom and came back with his gold-coin collection. "Daddy, can we give this to help those little kids?" I accepted it and sent the cash equivalent to a doctor friend who was serving in Ethiopia. Tiger doesn't know it, but I still have those gold coins. One day, when the time is right, I'll give them back to him and recall that moment, which brought tears to my eyes.

Food has to taste good, look good, and smell good to be good. Collard greens, contrary to what Fuzzy Zoeller said, don't fit the bill.

I love golf, but my first love was baseball. I was a catcher. When I was twelve,

Roy Campanella and Satchel Paige came through town on a barnstorming tour. They let me be the batboy because my dad was the scorekeeper. While they were warming up, I asked Roy if I could catch Satchel. He handed me his mitt and said, "Don't hurt yourself, boy." I said, "Don't worry. I've got a major-league arm." Campanella giggled at that. I said, "By the way, tell Satch that after he throws his last pitch, he'd better duck, because I'm gonna throw the ball right through his chest." Roy just shook his head.

Satch's first pitch came in real easy. I threw it back harder than he threw it to me. Satch threw the next one harder. So did I. By the time he threw his last warm-up pitch, he was really bringing it. And when I caught it, I sprang out of my crouch and threw it right where Satchel's chest was. You better believe he got out of the way. The second baseman caught the ball ankle high, on the right-hand side of the bag. Roy said, "Boy, you really do have a major-league arm."

I did have a good arm. And I can say that I caught the great Satchel Paige.

My mother insisted that I speak in good, clear English. No sloughing off on my *es*, *f*s and *t*s. Learn good grammar. If I had said "ax" when I meant "ask," she would have been all over my case. Today, I concur with Thurgood Marshall—there is nothing wrong with speaking the language of your culture when you're within that culture. But to be upwardly mobile in society, one must learn to speak the best English that one can.

Yes, Tiger is known to swear on the course. You can't have it both ways. You can't have the fire, intensity, competitiveness, and aggressiveness if you don't blow off steam. Profanity is the language of youth. I don't say it's right; I just say that's the way it is.

Before I left for my second tour of Vietnam, the Army assigned a demolitions expert to me. This man was an expert at hurting people, and he loved his work. He was a genius at creating special booby traps and tripwires, all sorts of custom devices to inflict maximum pain and damage. It's all he talked about. We'd send him out to prepare a perimeter, and in an hour he'd come back with a look of great satisfaction. "Nobody's coming through there, sir," he'd say, and I knew he meant it. I was glad he was on our side, but eventually I was glad to get away from him. He scared the hell out of me.

The secret to being a good player is balance. I don't mean keeping your equilibrium. I mean placing an equal emphasis on driving, iron play, short game, and putting. It's the most obvious thing, but very few players have balance. And almost nobody works to correct it.

Most people cannot or will not discuss their combat experiences. It's too traumatic and painful. I saw all the things you see in war—dead bodies, brains all over the place, friends dying—and I can talk about it. I had a mind-set that this was war, and that it doesn't make a lot of sense, but I had a job to do. I didn't overanalyze it. I loved myself too much to let it take something away from me.

Many times I've been in bed and it's one a.m. and I'm tired but don't want to go to sleep because I don't want the day to end. My goal is to enjoy every minute of every day, squeeze every bit out of it that I can. I have a hard time looking ahead because I'm so involved with what's going on right now. I love living life.

To a golfer at Tiger's level, a good caddie is as important as a good wife. There has to be a chemistry between the two, and the caddie must have great technical ability. There cannot be one shred of doubt in the player's mind that what the caddie is suggesting is correct. Some people think the caddie is overrated. I see it just the opposite.

Many years ago I attended a self-help seminar. One exercise concerned money. They asked us to write down the material things we desired to have in a two-week period. Then what we wanted in a month, three months, six months, a year, and five years down the road. I forgot about the seminar, and ten years later, I accidentally came across my lists. I laughed, because I had everything I'd wanted. On the list was a sports car. Well, I had two. I also put down that I wanted $10,000 in the bank. I had a lot more than that. These things seemed as far away as the moon when I wrote them down. They in fact were right around the corner.

The Bible says the love of money is the root of all evil, but I'm not so sure. There are a lot of poor countries with all the evil you'd want. The desire for power is much more corruptive.

The worst part of getting older is realizing what you could have accomplished if you'd known then what you know now. Every old person, no matter how content they seem, feels that sense of regret. It's a bitch, but it's part of life. So be nice to me.

I acquired some knowledge of geopolitics through my two tours of Vietnam. I can unequivocally say that as hairy as things are in Iraq, the situation would be apocalyptic if we pulled out. Civil war, reprisals, and bloodshed like you can't imagine. I support our involvement there totally, for humanitarian reasons. At a minimum.

Listen to Tiger when he loses. He does it graciously. He acknowledges that the other guy was the better golfer that day. The one thing he doesn't say is that the other guy was better overall.

Tiger has tried all kinds of creative ways to get me to give up cigarettes. I appreciate that, but he might as well be talking to a tree. We have an understanding. When our plane lands in Hong Kong, Tiger gets the baggage. I go to the curb and smoke.

Tiger and I were in our motel at a junior tournament. He was eleven. Out of the blue he asked, "What's male menopause?" We talked about it for an hour. Then he asked, "What's the immigration policy of Australia?" That took another hour. Tiger then said, "Dad, what's…" I didn't let him finish. I put his butt in bed.

There's one thing about my smoking that Tiger has either forgotten or never listened to in the first place. I don't inhale.

Jack Nicklaus

Jack has always been underrated as an interview subject. If you ask questions that challenge him or tickle his imagination, he will say more in a short period of time than almost anyone in golf. The setting for my interview with Jack was unusual; I flew to his offices in West Palm Beach and boarded his private plane en route to Hawaii. He dropped me off in El Paso, Texas, where he stopped to refuel. It was some three-hour flight; we touched on a dizzying number of topics, including baseball, movies, the nightly news, his having polio as a child, his parents, and his youth. He was terrific on the game itself, of course, and his thoughts on learning and playing were priceless. It was without question one of the most enjoyable flights of my life.

○ ○ ○

I had polio when I was thirteen. I started feeling stiff, my joints ached, and over a two-week period I lost my coordination and twenty pounds. The doctors thought I had the flu. I played an exhibition with Patty Berg and shot 53 for nine holes—not very good for a kid with a plus-three handicap. My sister, Marilyn, was diagnosed at about the same time; the doctors deduced that she got it from me. Marilyn, who was ten, was unlucky. For a year she was unable to walk but eventually got 95 percent of her movement back. I recovered after a few weeks, but I still may suffer from post-polio syndrome. My whole career, my joints have gotten awfully sore at times. Polio is just a memory now, but it was a horrible disease. I got it a year or two before Jonas Salk's polio vaccine was distributed.

My favorite team was the Columbus Redbirds. They were a farm team for the St. Louis Cardinals, and their best pitcher was Harvey Haddix, who later pitched twelve perfect innings for the Pittsburgh Pirates. Harvey signed a baseball for me, and I kept it as a keepsake for many years. One day the ball disappeared, then mysteriously turned up again, beat up and caked with mud. I never did discover what happened to that baseball, though I think a ten-year-old boy named Steve Nicklaus had something to do with it.

I'd rather be two strokes ahead going into the last day than two strokes behind. Having said that, it's probably easier to win coming from behind. There is no fear in chasing. There is fear in *being* chased.

I always liked to visit a major-championship site early. One reason was to prepare, but I also enjoyed taking my boys along and having them play with me. It was a blast watching one of my kids who, say, was an 82-shooter, try to break 90 on a U.S. Open golf course. I enjoyed it more than they did.

In 1972 I took the Masters and the U.S. Open, then came close to winning the British Open. I've been asked how I would have done at the PGA if somehow I'd come through in the British. Well, when I arrived home from Scotland that year, I went and got a haircut and a manicure. A manicure, for heaven's sake, the only one I ever had in my life. And I developed an infection in my right forefinger that required surgery. It hurt, and I had a big bandage. I played the PGA with my right forefinger off the club. [Nicklaus tied for thirteenth.] So I'm not saying I couldn't have won the PGA, because I'm sure I would have loved the pressure. But that darned manicure wouldn't have made it very easy.

Try a softer, more flexible shaft. At the U.S. Open at Oak Hill in 1968, I used a shaft in my driver that was between "R" and "S." I never could use an extra-stiff shaft; I couldn't feel the clubhead and as a result tried to overpower the ball with my hands and arms.

When Jock Hutchison and Freddie McLeod were the honorary starters at the Masters, for years they hit more than one shot. They'd play all eighteen holes. It's been suggested that the next honorary starters, whoever they are, should keep playing for a while. Nine holes maybe, just to give the fans a chance to watch these legends play. It's an intriguing idea, and if you're asking if I'd be interested in doing that, the answer is no.

When I fly in a helicopter, I insist there be two sets of controls, one for me in case something happens to the pilot. I'm no expert, but I know enough to at least get the thing on the ground. Nothing scares me like the thought of not being in control.

I take that back. MRI tubes confine you so much they scare me, just like they scare a lot of people. A friend of mine had an MRI, and when he was finished, he went right to his lawyer and changed his will. He chose to be cremated instead of buried.

At twenty-one, I was making $24,000 a year. That was pretty big money for a kid in those days. I made $12,000 selling insurance, $6,000 working for a slacks company and $6,000 more playing customer golf for the slacks manufacturer. Had I kept on at those things, I would have been miserable. The chance to make money was not a factor in my decision to turn pro, because I already had enough money. Heck, my first house cost only $22,000. All I ever wanted to do was play competitive golf against the best players in the world.

At my best, I hit three or four perfect shots a round. Can you do better than that? Probably not. So take an extra club for your second shot. If you're in between clubs, take the longer club, choke down a little and make a full, aggressive swing. That's better than not choking down and swinging easier, which may cause you to decelerate.

Swing the long irons as though they all have NO. 7 stamped on the sole. If you swing the 3-iron like you do the 7-iron, you won't swing too hard or try to help the ball in the air—which is the tendency with long irons.

It's very important to lose graciously. My dad taught me that. The guy who won had to be pretty good to beat you, right? So give him credit, and mean it.

Spanking your children these days is frowned upon. That to me is ridiculous. Giving your child an occasional little smack on the rear end—and I want to emphasize I don't mean a beating—is an acceptable way to get your point across. It's not the pain that makes it effective. It's the anticipation of getting spanked, the noise of it, and the fact you're unhappy that makes an impression, not the spanking itself.

I never saw a single episode of *M*A*S*H*. I've never seen *Cheers* or *Seinfeld*. The only show remotely like them I watch is *24*. Gary [son] got his wife some episodes for Christmas and brought them on the boat, and I got hooked. Other than that, my favorite program is *SportsCenter*. I especially like it in the morning, when they air last night's show four times, back to back.

Even the news is hard for me to watch; the media seems obsessed with nailing President Bush every single day. In a country where someone dies of diabetes every three minutes, the attacks on him wear me out. Where's the balance?

Barbara and I went to see a movie the other night that was depressing. I'm sure it'll win all sorts of Academy Awards, but it wasn't my cup of tea. Why are these movies that "make you think" always depressing? I want to laugh, or more important, I want to be entertained. Give me a movie like *Something's Gotta Give* or *Anger Management* or *Caddyshack* any day.

I go to church only a few times a year. Barbara is giving me a look as I say this, but darn it, I pray every day and worship in my own way. I just never got in the habit of going. Remember, I spent the better part of my life working on Sundays.

I don't carry a cell phone, never will. Anyone ever call to give you anything?

I don't believe in luck. Not in golf, anyway. There are good bounces and bad bounces, sure, but the ball is round and so is the hole. If you find yourself in a position where you hope for luck to pull you through, you're in serious trouble.

You've got to eliminate self-doubt. Self-doubt stinks.

My last thought before I take the club away isn't a thought at all. It's a picture, a visualization, a sensation. If I think of swinging slowly, my last thought isn't "swing slowly." It's an image of me swinging slowly.

If you slice, try keeping your left shoulder stationary on the downswing. It won't stay still, of course, but it will stop you from spinning your shoulders to the left and coming over the top.

When you get in position to putt, set your head and eyes so you can glance at the hole without swiveling your head. Your eyes are riveted on the ball when you make the stroke and your head must be kept still, but you also want to be target-oriented.

I putted with my glove on because I didn't want to remove it eighteen times a round.

If you're not putting well, shorten your stroke and hit the ball more firmly. Gordon

Jones [a fellow competitor] gave me that tip just prior to the 1967 U.S. Open, and it made the angels sing. I won the championship.

As you know, there's no use trying to get rid of a song that's stuck in your head. When you get to the first tee, you can only hope it's a good one. I've played very well to Harry Belafonte singing "Jamaica Farewell." And it's hard to play badly to "Raindrops Keep Falling on My Head."

Lloyd Mangrum had the reputation for being one of the toughest golfers ever. I remember when I was ten years old, I went in the locker room at Scioto to get an autograph, and there was Lloyd, playing cards, sitting there with a cigarette hanging from his mouth. He looked at me and barked, "What do you want, kid?" I was like anyone would be at the moment, and was taken aback by Lloyd's gruffness. I was only ten at the time, but that stuck with me.

Lloyd's wife, Aleta, might have had a greater influence on my wife, Barbara, than any other person. At the 1962 Masters, I was on the course and Barbara was on the veranda, bemoaning that she missed her baby. Jackie, our oldest, was only about seven months old at the time. All of a sudden, a woman who had been knitting looked up and said, "Look here, little girl. You had Jack long before you had that baby, and you hope to have him long after that baby is gone. So grow up and be a wife." Case closed! Ten years later, Barbara saw Aleta and told her, "You'll never know what you did for my marriage." It isn't easy being the wife of a professional athlete, and Barbara has told this story to other tour wives over the years.

When I won the 1994 Mercedes Championships, I received $100,000 and a new car. On one hand, I had an endorsement deal with Lincoln-Mercury, and the class of Mercedes I won was in direct competition with a line made by the company I represented. On the other hand, Mercedes had put up a great deal of money to sponsor the event. So I traded the car, which cost $30,000, for an $85,000 model, one that didn't compete with Lincoln-Mercury. I paid the $55,000 difference. Both car companies were happy. A year later, I sold the car, which I never drove, for exactly $55,000—there was depreciation, and I cut the guy a deal. I joke today that for what I paid flying my private plane that year, paying the taxes on the new car along with the difference in base cost, taking care of my caddie and other expenses, I came away from the 1994 Mercedes Championships $50,000 in the red. That's an exaggeration of course, but somewhere in there is a small lesson on money versus principles.

I was against giving Casey Martin a cart. You ask, "What if he were your own son?" and my answer is, "What's bigger, an individual or the game of golf?" In truth, the case ended perfectly. Casey, who is a terrific young man and a friend of mine, got to pursue his dream. Meanwhile, the prohibition against carts and the status of golf as a walking game remained intact.

I have a feeling I'll be playing tennis long after I quit playing golf. Golf is much harder on me physically than tennis is.

I'm not much of a drinker at all. Today, I might have three beers over the course of a year, if that. Sure, when I was younger, I was like a lot of college kids. I tried to drink all the beer in Columbus, Ohio. Barbara is giving me that look again.

And I could eat! At Lafayette, Louisiana, where they played the Cajun Classic in the early '60s, I'd go crazy for oysters. There's a picture of me from that period hoisting a big forkful of oysters into my mouth. I put away eight dozen oysters, went back to the hotel and changed, then went out to dinner, where I ate two dozen more oysters before the entree arrived. Yes, I could put the food away.

During Hell Week at Ohio State, for breakfast each day they made us eat a garlic bud, tie an onion around our neck, and eat a few goldfish to tide us over for the day. This stayed with you all day long, as you can imagine. The heartburn alone was unbelievable. And by the way, there's not much of a taste with goldfish—just a little bitter.

Woody Hayes lived a block and a half from my dad's pharmacy. He knew I played several sports and that I especially loved football. I was a quarterback, linebacker, and placekicker, and in practice could kick a field goal from fifty yards. I dreamed of playing football at Ohio State. My dad, who played some professional football and knew quite a bit about the sport, once asked Woody for advice about me. Woody said, "Football is a great game, but I know the talents of your son in golf. Keep him as far away from my game as you can." He didn't say I couldn't make the team at Ohio State. He only implied that golf was my best game and that I should focus on that. So I stuck with golf and basketball the remainder of high school.

When Barbara's mother died, Woody came by the funeral home. The atmosphere was sad, but a ways into it I look over, and there's Woody in a corner with my four boys. I walk over, and he's giving them a lesson on military history, deflecting the sadness. I was thinking how thoughtful that was when Barbara gets a phone call. It was Woody's wife, wanting to know if Woody was there. She asked if he had his walker with him and whether his car was in the parking lot. It turned out Woody had just had a stroke and wasn't supposed to be out of the house, let alone not have his walker or try to drive a car. But he wanted to be there for Barbara and the boys and snuck away to be there. Woody's legacy is mixed, but in my opinion he was a great man.

If a cell phone or camera going off disrupts you, you've got issues with concentration on your golf game. If you're totally absorbed in the shot you're playing, how can you hear anything?

My dreams are productive. Many times I've been near the lead in a golf tournament, despite having trouble with some part of my game. I can't seem to fix the problem, no matter how many balls I hit or how much thought I give it. Then I'll go to bed and dream I'm working on the problem, and when I wake up, I have the answer. Usually it's something small, like my eye alignment or weight distribution.

Gary Player likes to say, "Jack is not only the best winner of all time, he's the best loser." The "best loser" part of that bugs me. It implies I'm adept at losing. I've asked Gary to substitute the word *gracious* for *best,* or just say "Jack is a good sport," but he won't do it. He gets too big a kick out of complimenting and teasing me at the same time.

There are more good players today. There were more great players in my day.

The PGA Tour's prohibition against players wearing shorts started when Jimmy Demaret wore a pair of very short shorts at the 1961 World Cup in Puerto Rico. When Jimmy stooped to line up putts, his shorts turned out to be very revealing. Now, I have no objection to the PGA Tour's mandate that players wear long pants. But I wear shorts 99 percent of the time, including when I go to the office, so I wouldn't object if knee-length shorts were permitted when the temperature gets around ninety degrees.

Friendships are valuable. If your partner is also your best friend, that's invaluable.

I just made Barbara smile.

Tom Weiskopf

In his heyday he was known as the "Towering Inferno" for his dark intensity and fuming nature, but I always thought it was misplaced. Weiskopf was never demonstratively angry to where he would, say, throw clubs. His infrequent brooding was almost always directed inward, his lingering dissatisfaction with his game too difficult to conceal. One of the most naturally gifted men ever to play the game, Weiskopf set an impossibly high standard for himself and was the victim of a perfectionist nature. He has mellowed and has come to terms with many things from his past—his shortcomings as a husband, his tendency to drink too much, his impatience with his game, and his failing to take care of a body that seemed to be designed for the express purpose of swinging a golf club. Weiskopf is intelligent, perceptive, and most of all, dead honest. I had written about him several times, most notably about his almost dying when he was caught in a peat bog in Scotland, and about his near-win at the 1975 Masters. They were fun stories but took a backseat to the *My Shot* we did together near his home in Scottsdale in 2002.

o o o

I can laugh at myself in some ways, but not when it comes to hitting bad shots. What's so funny about a shank?

I went to a Catholic high school. One day in chemistry class, a few of us took a silver dollar and heated it over a Bunsen burner until it almost glowed. Then we put it on an empty chair and asked a poor, unsuspecting kid, "Hey, is that your dollar?" Of course, it burned the kid's fingers when he tried to pick it up, which we thought was hilarious. But we didn't think it was funny for long. Within fifteen minutes a priest was beating my bare backside with a hairbrush. I came away much worse off than the kid who picked up the silver dollar. To this day, I have a great respect for priests.

The PGA Tour entertains people, helps them escape. I played a game for a living, but there was value in that. If all you thought about was your job, the economy, sick kids, and terrorism, you'd go out of your mind.

My favorite actor? I've got to go with Clayton Moore. When I was little, the Lone Ranger dominated my life. The mask, the silver bullets, his friendship with Tonto, the little sermon at the end of each episode.

That was very strong stuff. "Hi-yo, Silver, away!"

My dad took me to the 1957 U.S. Open at Inverness when I was fourteen. I wasn't a golfer yet. After we walked through the gate, he took me straight to the practice range and pointed out Sam Snead. The sound of Sam's iron shots, the flight of the ball, thrilled me. I was hooked even before I started playing.

The perfectionist who tries to play golf for a living usually ends up saying to hell with it. I'm a perfectionist, and I had some success, but only because I was persistent and had some talent. In the end, the game ate me up inside, and I retired earlier than a lot of guys do. Perfectionists are determined to master things, and you can never master golf.

I stopped drinking eighteen months ago. It was a serious problem for many years. It ruined my career. Every big mistake I've made can be traced back to drinking.

The most persistent feelings I have about my career are guilt and remorse. Sometimes they almost overwhelm me. I'm proud I won fifteen times on tour and the 1973 British Open. I should have won twice that many, easy. I wasted my potential. I didn't utilize the talent God gave me.

Nothing cures a hangover like a milkshake followed by a cheeseburger, the greasier the better. First you drink the milkshake; it coats your stomach, and the sugar does you good. Then you eat the cheeseburger, slowly. The grease helps replace oxygen in your blood, the bread soaks up whatever's left of the alcohol, and the whole thing sits well in your stomach.

All things in moderation? Damn, that's hard to do.

My friendship with Bert Yancey taught me how helpless a person with mental illness can be. Here was a brilliant man with a genius for golf, who was rendered almost useless by his manic-depressive condition. He taught me to have compassion for those who aren't as strong or healthy as you are.

Tour pros would rather go through an IRS audit than play in a pro-am. Publicly they say they love meeting interesting people and how great the pro-ams are. In truth, they loathe them. They're out there for six hours, see countless bad shots, and hear the same stale jokes. If Tim Finchem announced next Monday that pro-ams were henceforth eliminated, he'd find two hundred cases of champagne on his porch Tuesday morning.

Ben Hogan had no calluses on his hands. The first time I shook his hand, I was amazed. His skin was tough as rawhide, but there was no buildup anywhere. That's a sign of how perfect his grip was. The fact he didn't wear a glove makes it even more amazing.

With beer and wine, you've got a chance. The high-test stuff, forget it.

My take on the Senior PGA Tour: The golf is good, the toupees are awful. I may be bald, but I'll never glue one of those divots on my head, and that's a promise.

I'll be damned if I can understand open-casket funerals.

I can't tell you how much I hated practicing my putting. It bored me silly. I loved to hit balls, though. Golfers tend to practice the things they're already good at.

My dad worked for the Newburgh & South Shore Railroad in Ohio. It was his job to hire and fire people; the stress it put on him was enormous. My dad was a sensitive man to begin with, and when he had to lay someone off he'd get depressed and go on a two-day drunk. The most terrible time of all came when he had to fire his best friend. There had been an accident in which a couple of people were killed, and my dad's friend was to blame. The guy was one year away from retirement and a full pension, and my dad fired him and the guy lost it all. This time my dad didn't get drunk for two days—he stayed drunk for three years.

I suppose it was a harder, black-and-white world back then. Me, I couldn't fire my best friend. I'd find a way to get the guy to retirement so he could get his pension. But for my dad it was a matter of doing the correct thing, which also was the hard thing.

I've thought about that forty-foot putt Jack Nicklaus made to beat me at the '75 Masters a thousand times. It went up a slope and broke into the middle of the hole, an absolutely unmakable putt. I refuse to believe luck or some cosmic force had anything to do with it, because you can't compete against those things. It was pure skill all the way.

If I had to answer yes or no, I'd say flying saucers exist. They've hovered but haven't landed. Why would they? If you were an alien and were smart enough to design a flying saucer, why would you come here?

When people say they dream of playing in the U.S. Open someday, what they're really saying is, they'd like to be good enough to play. Trust me, the U.S. Open is not fun.

Going head-to-head against Jack Nicklaus in a major was like trying to drain the Pacific Ocean with a teacup. You stand on the first tee knowing that your very best golf might not be good enough. You experience a sagging sort of pressure that just gets worse as the day wears on. The last four holes are always murder—the crowds, the difficulty of the golf course, the fatigue, the realization that Jack is not going to make a mistake—all of it hits you at once. Jack would get this look on his face that expressed deep suspicion in your ability to handle this, and in the end I rarely could.

Letter writing has become a lost art. Even the sweetest letters I get nowadays look rushed, and the penmanship isn't good. The British haven't lost their touch, though. Letters that land from Scotland and England are always elegant, thoughtful, and beautiful. What have they got that we haven't?

The neatest thing about playing was my ability to surprise myself. Under pressure sometimes I'd face a real hard shot I'd never played before and pull it off just the way I envisioned it. It's a superhuman feeling. But I'll tell you something about these great shots players hit: A lot of times they end up close to the hole by accident. There's a good chance they didn't hit the shot the way they planned it. Only the player knows how good or bad a shot really was.

It's customary to say, "Good luck; play well" to your playing partners before you tee off. I always thought, "Thanks, that's very nice, but piss on luck."

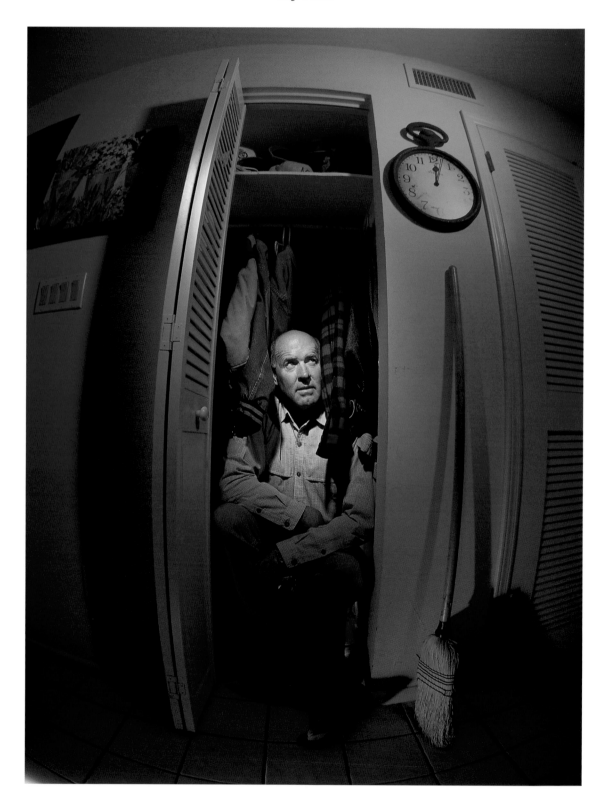

If you wonder whether you have a drinking problem, you do.

My advice to Ty Tryon: Do not, under any circumstances or for any amount of money, play with a set of clubs you don't absolutely love. Find a set you like better than any other and use them until you wear them out. And make sure you have an identical backup set ready for when the first set is trashed.

Jeanne and I divorced last year. It was my fault. My drinking led to behaviors that made me very unhappy with my life in general, and she was in the line of fire. Giving up alcohol has cleared my thinking, given me a new perspective, brought me to some realizations. Fortunately there is no animosity between the two of us. We talk and see each other often. She's the finest person I've ever met and has always been my biggest cheerleader.

My most prized possession? Some time ago I went over to Jeanne's to pick up some stuff. One box was particularly heavy and rattled when I shook it. I went home and opened it, and lo and behold, it was my Lionel train set I had when I was a kid. The set was in unbelievable condition. All the cars were in their original boxes, the pieces of track bunched together just the way I left them fifty years ago. Only the transformer was a mess. I took the whole thing to a hobby shop in Montana to be reconditioned. When the guy saw what I had, he almost fainted. He said the boxes alone were worth a small fortune.

The set wasn't new when I received it. My dad got it for Christmas when he was young, and he passed it on to me. I never passed it along to my son, Eric, because I forgot I had it. But I'm going to pass it on to my first grandson, whenever he comes along. The train isn't for display. I'll tell him the story behind it, let him know who his great-grandfather was, help him put it together. Then we'll get down on the floor and play with it.

Nick Faldo

When I met Nick Faldo at La Costa in early 2006, his TV career had just gotten into full swing. Sitting down with a chatty Faldo was an arresting experience in view of his phlegmatic way of going when he was the best player in the world for a long stretch during the 1980s and early '90s. The sense was that Faldo was opening up too late. But better late than never, and my two hours with Faldo were like meeting a recluse who had just come out of hiding. Funny, witty, ironic, and half-apologetic for the aloofness he felt he had to display when he was the best golfer extant, he was good fun. Let's not forget either how great Faldo was: He won three Masters, three British Opens, and along with Seve Ballesteros was an anchor for a fleet of European Ryder Cup teams.

After winning six majors, he had some intriguing thoughts on TV, ghosts, aliens, and his prospects at fifty.

o o o

When I flew into the country a while back, the customs officer, who obviously was a golfer, recognized me. I hadn't filled in the window listing my occupation, and he wrote "sports analyst." I said, "Why not just write 'golfer'? What about the six majors?" He said quietly, "We both know what you do best these days." Couldn't argue with him there—though I wanted to.

ESPN called on behalf of Michael Jordan last year and said, "We'd really like to have you at Michael's tournament in the Bahamas." I said, "I'd love to. I'd swim there to play with Michael." The executive paused and said, "Not as a player, Nick. We need an announcer." I'm telling you, those majors feel like they happened a million years ago.

There are some secrets you'll never get out of me. The biggest is the strategy we Europeans use in foursomes during the Ryder Cup. It's one area of the Ryder Cup we've dominated, and this strategy really is the reason we've won four of the last five Ryder Cups. Tony Jacklin invented it, and it's beautiful in its simplicity and devastating in terms of its effectiveness in the alternate-shot format. If the Americans got wind of it, there would go the Ryder Cup. It's subtle, but very visible when you look at it head-on. An observant person can see it.

On the other hand, when I told Greg Norman, "Don't let the bastards get you down" on the last green at the 1996 Masters, that was a secret I knew had a statute of limitations. When it comes to history, you eventually want to set the record straight. So into my book it went, and nobody was the worse for wear.

As a boy, I was a hothead. Threw clubs up trees and carried on when things weren't going right. Then, in 1977, I missed a shot during a tournament and buried a club in the ground. Gerald Micklem, the former chairman of the R&A Championship Committee, saw me do it and walked over. I expected a real tongue-lashing, but he said, "I used to do that, and it never did me any good." Then he walked away. That was very powerful. I was embarrassed by what I did and really humbled by the way Mr. Micklem handled it. I got mad after that, but no more losing my temper.

I had only one sporting hero growing up: Björn Borg. He never argued with the umpires or got into it with other players. Strong. Quiet. Absolutely prepared for anything. Tough mentally. Played the fifth set the same as the first set. No ebb and flow emotionally. Four or five years ago, it occurred to me that I had subconsciously modeled myself after him.

Finally, after years of idolizing Borg, I met him. He played an exhibition against John McEnroe at Buckingham Palace, and I was introduced. I said, "Do you know you've been my hero for the last twenty-five years? It is a great privilege." His reaction? He just nodded, like he'd just won a point in the first set.

Golf on TV in Great Britain is characterized by showing lots of shots of the countryside or a nearby loch. It's much more pastoral, suited for the people at home drinking tea and eating scones. It can be too slow; in Barcelona once, they showed three players walking onto a green, and all three players three-putted. The camera didn't leave the green once. With due respect to that production style, I'm partial to the bang-bang style we have here in America.

It helps to be different, and in my case I do it without trying: I have a British accent. Americans love a British accent, and golf audiences really love it. I play on that, obviously. I'm not above saying, "Of course, old chap, I do say, jolly good," and so on.

Note to the TV networks: This boy has it all. I can be serious and analytical. Or philosophical, or dramatic. I'm quick and always good for a laugh. And I play nice with the others. I want to work, and you know where to reach me. But please phone on Thursday—I'm busy on weekends.

Listen to your heart and your gut. That small voice inside you. How often have you left the house knowing you've forgotten something and it turns out you have? Intuition is very powerful, and certainly it's true in golf. The young person tends to fight intuition, whereas people my age learn to go with it.

Can't figure women out, eh? You must accept that on virtually every issue you are not right—she is. That is the key to peace and happiness. I'm always mindful of something a friend once told me: "When I'm out walking in the woods, all alone, I'm still wrong."

I appreciate that my apparent personality transformation is hard to grasp. Certainly in my better playing days I kept my head down and the blinkers on, never showing my cards. *Get out of my way!* But I had to do it that way. I tried to be funny and entertaining a couple of times, but a few bogeys later, enough of that. The Hogan in me won out over the Peter Jacobsen in me.

When I was a boy, we had a little gang that played every day. I lived in a small house, two rooms up and two down, and across the street were some woods. It was our explorer area, and five of us lived in those woods. All day long we'd be over there, making up fantasy games, wars, and so on, lots of quests with elaborate plots. When we got older we left the woods and took to riding bicycles, and we wore out the streets of that town. I would disappear and not come back until the food was on the table. There is a lot to be said for that sort of rough-and-tumble upbringing, but sad to say, that time has come and gone. Can you imagine turning your children loose for ten hours without checking in on them?

Favorite movie? That's a tough one, but the Austin Powers movies come to mind. A bit part in one would go a long way to making me an even happier man. Just one line. You know the producer?

When I decided to totally rework my swing in 1985, I would begin hitting balls early in the morning, and I'd hit five of those very large baskets of balls—the kind they use to fill the little baskets—until, by about three o'clock in the afternoon, I couldn't close my hands anymore. Five of those baskets amounts to 1,500 balls, and my hands would just turn into claws. I would go off and have a swim, and then, when the sun was going down and it would cool off, I would go back and hit some more.

The reworking took two years. I've kept much of that experience to myself. It was dark, intense, and sometimes negative, wondering when the changes were going

to take—and if they would take. It is amazing really, with the stress I put my body through, that I didn't ruin my back, tear a rotator cuff, develop tendinitis, or any number of things. Using new muscles in my hips and other places, I would get so sore I felt crippled. Later I was bothered by tendinitis, as early as when I won the British Open in 1990. The worst area: the "snuffbox" on my left hand, that little pocket at the base of the thumb and forefinger. At the '90 Open, my snuffbox was so sore I hit all my iron shots in practice using a tee. Everyone thought it was some new kind of practice technique, when in fact I couldn't take a divot.

By late 1986 I had begun losing sponsors and endorsements. I'd gone from being nearly the best player in the world to not being able to hit my hat. I wasn't invited to play in the 1987 Masters, but that week I was in a satellite event. I'd been working on a little thing in my downswing, and, just like that, it clicked. I shot four 67s, finished second. I won in Spain in May, won the British Open at Muirfield in July, and at the end of the season, I knew I was on my way.

It's all about the "bottle," the British term meaning the ability to be in a situation and feel comfortable, be in control and have the mental toughness to get the job done. Great champions have the bottle almost all the time. Some have the bottle at isolated moments, others find it only once in a career, and others never find it.

The best player I saw at a given moment was Seve Ballesteros at Lytham in 1988. His charisma and confidence were so high, and the way he played was transcendent. I remember thinking that no man could have beaten him; there was a force that wouldn't allow it.

My goal was to be the No. 1 player in the world, and I did that. All was good and well, I was happy, and I remained motivated for quite some time. But something happens with that motivation. You work hard, and you aim for those goals anyway, but it lingers in you that you're not paying the true price necessary to give those goals their best chance of coming off.

Fanny Sunesson was and is one of the great caddies of all time. I was the world's No. 1 with her, and with the crowds and everything closing in on you, you need a strong personality at your side. You'd be surprised at how often caddies choke and can't give the player the correct yardages, and otherwise start stumbling and fumbling around. There was none of that with Fanny. She had the yardages spot on, and she handled the galleries with great authority. "Stand back!" she'd shout. "Quiet please!" I always smiled at how readily people obeyed her. Her physical stamina was amazing; I had a small fruit store in my bag that weighed more than thirty pounds, and the nature of the course was irrelevant; she never got tired.

When I was twenty, I moved to a little English village, to a place next door to a pub they said was at least six hundred years old. The pub truly was haunted. Many a time, nobody would be behind the bar, and bottles would fly off the shelves. Not fall, but fly across the room. It happened so often that the employees were used to it and only got mad that they had to sweep up the glass. The last house I had in England had a ghost cat. I never saw it, but the housekeeper said she saw a gray shadow go slinking across the floor near two of our pet cats, and when they saw the shadow, they would run from the room as though a bomb had gone off.

Then there are the aliens they have hidden in Roswell. When I saw President Clinton, I asked him about it, and I couldn't get a word out of him about it. Imagine that.

My big motivation now is to play the Champions Tour next year. Like everybody else, I had no great designs on playing it, but last year I decided to go for it and give it my best. You're only fifty once.

The alternate-shot secret, I'm keeping to myself. But I will say this about the four-ball: You need a good partner. There's no way around that, and I've had several. I started out with Peter Oosterhuis—he was my wing man, nailing down solid pars while I fired the big guns. Then Langer, Woosie, Monty, and finally, Lee Westwood. By the time I got to Monty, I was the wing man. You want the young guy to be relaxed and playing as loosely as possible, while the more experienced player is charged with being the glue. That's a bit of strategy I reveal at the European team's peril: Formulate every team knowing one guy is the wing man and the other is the main gunner.

Isn't it odd how you can see someone in a room, and you like them even before you're introduced? Once in a while, I'm just drawn to a person. My best friends in the world, I liked them immensely before I met them.

Early in my professional career, I had a best friend who also was a golfer. One night the phone rang, and it was him. He started reviewing his round with me, and on the second hole I put the phone down and made a sandwich, taking my time. When I picked up the phone, he was on the fourteenth hole and didn't know I'd ever left. That made an impression on me. Ever since, I've never had a best friend inside golf. I just don't want to talk about golf in the evenings. Furthermore, I'm competing against them, it's a business, and I don't want to give anything away. I have three or four close friends, a couple of whom I've known for twenty-five years or more. People I tell my secrets to, and I'd be there for them in a minute if they needed it.

Sometimes I'll launch into a story about something that happened to me during a championship, and a short way into it, the listener's eyes begin to glaze over. The story might be one I've never told before, and I think it's quite interesting, but then it hits me: That was twenty-five years ago. I need some new material.

Doug Sanders

A visit to Doug Sanders's house in Houston is like visiting a swinger's pad, circa 1968. There is kitsch everywhere, odd bits of memorabilia including an astronaut's suit, photographs signed by every notable film and TV star of the '60s, and framed displays of golf gloves worn by the greats and near-greats of the decades in which Sanders flourished. His closet contains a hundred or more pairs of his neon-colored golf shoes, most of them thirty years old and sporting the buckles and straps in vogue back then. It's not an unpleasant house. But it's...odd.

The *My Shot* series had to include Sanders. He was always a bit of an under-achiever, a genius driver and wedge player who won a lot of tournaments but never the big titles. He was a party guy who may have dissipated to excess, and physically the last twenty years have been so-so for him. But he's an excellent host and engaging company, spinning fantastic stories of his rise from stark poverty in rural Georgia to become one of the better players of his era. Sanders' peers view him as a case of what might have been, but he crammed two lifetimes of experiences into one, and his reminiscences made for fascinating listening.

○ ○ ○

I missed a thirty-inch putt on the last green that would have won the 1970 British Open. It's all anybody wants to talk about. I won twenty times on the PGA Tour, and if you gave me one birdie, four pars, and a bogey wherever I could put them, I'd have five majors. But it's that putt everybody remembers. What can I say? It's what I remember most, too.

The cardinal sin in match play is to get complacent. The way to avoid that is to be cruel. You want to step on your opponent's throat and enjoy it while you're doing it.

Don't let 'em up. Beat them as badly as possible. Even if your opponent is a nice guy, imagine that he wants to humiliate you, and give it back double.

We were too poor to make it. My dad walked five miles to work in Cedartown, Georgia, for fifty cents a day. There wasn't enough to eat. No doctors. Lice in our hair. Ratty hand-me-down clothes. So many people in the Depression had it like that. The strange thing is, nobody complained. Everybody just floated through it, waiting for the nightmare to end.

I started out caddieing at a nine-hole course. I wanted to play so badly. One day the pro, Maurice Hudson, said I could hit balls over by a hedge, so long as I was careful. I'd hit a ball, then place the next ball at the very edge of the divot I'd just taken. I'd do this over and over until I'd made one long, twenty-yard divot. I'd fix them, then start a new strip.

I chipped and putted for nickels and dimes against older guys, grown men. I never won. They chided me. "Come on, sucker," they'd say. They'd clean me out and I'd walk home in the dark, depressed and discouraged. The lightning bugs flashed around me; they looked like ghosts. I had to quit playing. But I'd show up at the course before the sun came up and practice. I'd practice more at night. Regardless of the weather, I was there. After three months of practice and no gambling, I showed up with five dollars and said, "Let's go." We chipped and putted, and I took all of their money. I walked home that night with twenty dollars in my pocket, the most money I'd ever had. The lightning bugs didn't look like ghosts anymore. They looked like stars.

I quit drinking ten years ago because it started going to my head more than it used to and was too hard on my body. All of my tricks—drinking a glass of milk every fourth cocktail to coat my stomach, for instance—didn't work anymore. Drinking is a young man's vice.

I wasn't a very good husband. I was a decent father, but domestic life was not my strong suit. I didn't lead a normal life. I was busy drinking, partying, chasing women, hitting balls, and running with Evel Knievel and the Rat Pack. I assumed there would be a few regrets, and I was right. But I also led the life I chose, so on balance I'm fine with being Doug Sanders.

I don't know of two people who did it more their way than me and my friend Frank Sinatra.

The more you get, the more you want.

Most of my career, I slept only four hours out of every twenty-four. I didn't need more than that. I could lie down and tell myself, eight minutes, conk out, and be deep asleep for those eight minutes. I'd wake up feeling pretty refreshed. I didn't want to sleep a third of my life away. For me, going to sleep was like ruining a good dream.

Picking cotton for a nickel a day when I was seven years old was murder. I hated it. The heat was intense, and the cotton hulls chewed up your hands something awful. It was just like the movie *Places in the Heart.* One day I decided to take a shortcut. What happened was, when they planted the cotton, they would plant several watermelons in the fields along with it. When the workers got thirsty, they'd bust open a watermelon and have at it. One day I buried a little runt watermelon deep in my sack to make it weigh more. I poured a little water on the cotton just for good measure. When they put my sack on the scale, the owner caught me immediately. He began his lecture with, "Son, your ass is gonna wear out before my size-thirteen shoe will." He forced me to work for him until all the cotton was in. It taught me a lesson about doing a job the right way. I also swore I'd never pick cotton again.

In a money game at Cedartown one day, a guy named Dallas Weaver found his ball behind a tree. A lot of money was riding.

We thought he was dead. There were train tracks running by our course, and just then a freight train came through. Dallas Weaver turned sideways, took some kind of low iron, and banked the ball off the side of a freight car and almost onto the green. That was fifty years ago, and I've never seen anyone top that shot.

The moonshine we made around Cedartown was not clear, like grain alcohol. It was the color of Coca-Cola. After I strained it through a tablecloth, it was the color of gasoline. It's about as powerful as gasoline, too, about 190 proof. I always kept a gallon or two of moonshine around for guests. They were very curious about it; most people have never tasted real moonshine.

I gave a small glass to Dean Martin once with the standard warning. "This is not like whiskey," I said. "Take tiny sips, or you'll be in for it." Dean was skeptical. He took a mouthful, swallowed half, and was ready to swallow the other half, when I went to light a cigarette. Dean's eyes got big, and he sprayed what was left of the moonshine on the floor. "Don't light that smoke!" he screamed. "You'll blow my head off!" My moonshine almost sent Dean Martin to his knees. It is not to be trifled with.

When my feel was good, I could snatch a fly out of the air with two toothpicks. When my touch was off, I was just another player. Once in a while my feel would desert me suddenly. One year in Orlando I opened 66–66 and had a four-shot lead. Yet, early in the third round, I knew I was going to be lucky to finish in the top ten. My touch was gone, and I knew there was nothing I could do about it. There's a lesson in this: When the train runs off the tracks, don't panic, because it'll just make it worse.

Three failed marriages taught me this: You can disagree with what a woman says, but never argue with how she feels.

You hear how Ben Hogan was a thoughtful, interesting, chatty person away from the golf course. I never saw that at all. I played with Ben a lot and was on the 1967 Ryder Cup team that he captained. The truth is, Hogan was the hardest person to talk to I ever met in my life.

In hot, humid weather I gave myself an edge: I shaved under my arms. Give it a try. You'll feel clean and classy. You'll be more comfortable. Your deodorant will work better, too.

Right now I'd love a glass of buttermilk. I crave it but can't find it anywhere. It's almost extinct, like the dinosaurs.

A no-tipping policy serves two purposes: It keeps the workers poor and denies the customer an opportunity to feel good about himself. Therefore, I ignore it.

Generosity is giving more than you can. Pride is taking less than you need. Jill St. John told me that. She got it from Kahlil Gibran.

Doug Ford had the best short game I ever saw. He was a tough guy. If I had asked him to teach me a couple of shots, he probably would have said, "Get out there and learn yourself, like I did." One night I took Doug down to a steakhouse. Got him a big steak for $3.95, ordered a couple of carafes of wine for $1.25 apiece. We got to laughing. The wine kicked in. "Tell me how you played that pitch on seventeen today," I said. "Well, first you weaken your grip," he said, and he went on to give me all kinds of secrets. I would have given him fifty dollars cash to teach me that shot, but I got it for under ten dollars and had a good meal to boot.

In the early 1960s very few of us had regular caddies. At a tournament you took the caddie they assigned you, and there were some beauties. Bobby Brue slipped ten dollars to the caddiemaster once, hoping he'd get a caddie who knew what he was doing. On the first hole, Bobby asked the guy how far it was to the hole. The caddie answers, "About three blocks."

Clothes make the man. You know how you go to a hardware store to buy paint and they have fifty shades of white? I went to great lengths to blend the colors of my clothes just right. I found my best color combinations at the pharmacy. I'd look at all the colorful medicine capsules, choose the ones I liked, then have the pharmacist dump out the medicine. I'd stick the top half of an empty yellow capsule onto the bottom half of a blue one, then send it to the factory where my shirts and slacks could be colored the same way. My wife would send my white underwear and socks along with the capsules so they could be dyed along with the other fabric. Oh, my clothes were beautiful. Still are.

Figure out how much you spend on clothing each year, then spend it in equal sums twice a year instead of in dribbles. Once a year, thin out your wardrobe. Give away what you don't need.

I had torticollis, a neck condition where my head tilted one way and my chin went the other. I couldn't hit a golf ball without biting the collar of my shirt to keep my head in place. The pain was terrible, like an intense cramp that never goes away. The doctor said he could operate for eight hours and probably straighten my head, but the chances of curing the pain were only fifty-fifty. I didn't want to live anymore. I started looking for a possible way out. I made a phone call, and a few days later my doorbell rings. The man at the door introduced himself as Tony and said he was there with orders to help. We worked out the details over dinner. We would go to a public place that wasn't crowded. In the parking lot there, when no one was around, Tony would put a bullet in my head. It would look like a robbery; I wanted to avoid the stigma of a suicide. There was the matter of how much the hit would cost. The rate Tony gave me was too low; I upped it to $40,000. For that kind of dough, I knew I could count on him to do the job right.

The operation was a success. A surgeon in Montreal straightened my head, and much of the pain was gone—though I still take pain pills. I called the man in charge and told him I wouldn't be needing Tony. He said congratulations, good luck, and if I needed him, I knew where to find him.

During my torticollis operation, my heart stopped beating. Suddenly I was walking barefoot on a grassy path. There were two small mountains to my left with a beautiful valley between them. Everything was illuminated, yet there was no sun. It was beautiful. I thought, *I made it!* Then there was a huge thump, and I was back on the operating table. For just a moment, I was disappointed to be back.

My brother, Ernest, was blind from age four. He picked up a dynamite cap in a coal yard and lit it with a splinter. Blew his fingers off and his eyes out. He was amazing. He would hitchhike from Cedartown to Macon and back; he could walk along the road and find his way home by sound and feel. His cane was like a long finger. He was an excellent guitar player, could rollerskate, and was a whiz at geography. Never forgot a name or a voice. It was almost like he was whole. After a while it was hard to feel sorry for Ernest, which is how most handicapped people want it anyway.

You won't learn a thing hanging out with drunks, dope addicts, and other asses. You got to be around winners. Some people never figure that out. I knew it by the time I was twelve.

Winners listen to other people. They're always trying to learn; they respect other people's opinions. Losers just want to talk.

I won a lot of money playing gin. I had a good memory, so I always knew what cards had been played. I could pay attention—did you know most people put all of their high cards on one side of their hand? And I had experience. If you have those three things, you can clean up. If you're missing just one, you should play for pennies or else stick with golf, because you'll wind up a pigeon.

If you want someone to be on time, don't tell them to be there at nine o'clock. Tell them to be there at 8:58. When you nail down an exact minute, it stays in their mind. They'll think, *This guy's precise.*

Like a lot of tour pros, I escaped a hundred speeding tickets. We left our driver's licenses in the trunk of the car. When you retrieved it for the highway patrolman, he'd see that big, shiny golf bag with your name on it. A dozen balls and a signed photograph, and you were on your way.

One time I couldn't talk my way out of the ticket. I had to pay thirty dollars on the spot. When I got back in the car, my son, Brad, who was six at the time, said, "What happened—you find someone who doesn't play golf?" I said, "Shut up."

If you feel your friends overlook the Christmas cards you send, do what a friend of mine does: Mail them in July.

If I could jump in a time machine and go back thirty years, I'd do it in a second. Golden years, my ass.

Bob Wilson

Midway through the series, I had yet to interview a subject who was not entrenched in the mainstream of golf. Golf has many peripheries, and rooting through them I was lucky to discover Bob Wilson. A double amputee who lost his legs on an aircraft carrier more than thirty years ago, Wilson has devoted much of his life to reaching out to those who are similarly disabled. Wilson is a brilliant and personable fellow whose plain manner of speaking reminded me of actor George Kennedy. He is passionate and dedicated to the National Amputee Golf Association, which in my opinion would have dissolved long ago were it not for his zeal. Eric Larson's photograph of Bob exploding through the ball, maintaining his balance beautifully on his prosthetic limbs, projected his can-do spirit wonderfully. Bob and I still talk on the phone frequently; his friendship is one of the happiest byproducts of the *My Shot* quest.

○ ○ ○

I asked the shoe attendant at the club if my loafers were shined and ready. "Which ones are yours?" he asked. "The ones that don't stink," I said.

Playing with me has its upsides and downsides. If your ball plunges into shallow water, I'll get it for you. If your ball stops near a rattlesnake, or if the cigar you tossed on the ground starts a small brush fire that needs stomping out, I'm your man. But if we're playing a scramble and we've got a sidehill or downhill lie, don't count on me to come through.

I was in line at a supermarket one day, and behind me is a mother and five-year-old child. I was wearing shorts, and the child, of course, had his eyes riveted on my prosthetics. Now, instead of covering the kid's eyes and hissing that he shouldn't stare, she let him look for a full minute. Then she leaned down and said in a stage whisper, "Isn't that cool?" The child looked a bit longer, then nodded. "That's real cool. Can I have some?" That just made my day. And it helped shape that kid's view of amputees for the rest of his life.

Here's how it happened. In 1974 I was a lieutenant commander in the Navy, in charge of the flight deck on the USS *Kitty Hawk*. We were running routine takeoff and landing exercises in the South China Sea. Anything that moved on the deck was my responsibility: I was a nut for safety and a hard-ass about it—I once grabbed a guy and ordered him to put on a vest and helmet, not knowing it was Red Dog Davis, the admiral of the fleet. But that's another story. One day we were particularly active. F-4 jets were coming in every two to three minutes. After a plane lands, it's vital that you get them out of the way quickly to make room for the other incoming planes.

One pilot who'd just landed wasn't following the director's signals to pivot his aircraft and clear out. I quickly stepped forward and took over because I knew the pilot and knew he would recognize me in my bright yellow flight-deck officer's shirt. You're supposed to maintain eye contact with the pilot as you move him around. In doing that, I inadvertently took three steps backward and stepped over the "foul deck line," the painted line that marks the area occupied by the large cables that grab the tailhooks on the aircraft and bring them to a stop. When a jet hits the deck, it's traveling 170 miles per hour—and so is the cable when it catches the jet. Within two seconds of stepping over the foul deck line, in came a jet, and off went my legs. Clean, just below the knees.

I came to in a hospital in the Philippines five days later. Being delirious, I started ripping the tubes out of my body. A nurse rushed in and said, "What are you doing?" I told her, "I'm going swimming. It's too damned hot in here." Another shot of morphine, and bam, I was out again. Next thing I know, I'm in a naval hospital in Philadelphia.

My first thought—every amputee's first thought—was, *What do I do now? How do I provide for my family?* I had a degree in economics from Fairleigh Dickinson, but I had no experience at it. Hell, I was a Navy guy. I was also old school. I had a wife, and my second child was born three weeks before the accident. My job is to provide. How do I support them? I ended up staying in the Navy. There was a lot of stress, a lot of worry, and, of course, indescribable pain physically. But I knew I would make it, because my family was there for me. Other guys, they had divorce papers waiting for them when they got home. I'll tell you, golf was way down the list.

But it was on the list. I had taken up the game at seventeen and was a four-handicap player. I'd played all over Hawaii and the Philippines. My clubs were on the carrier the day I lost my legs. In the hospital one day, I pick up a copy of *Golf World*, and on the cover was a photograph of Bic Long, who had just won the National Amputee Golf Association championship at Pinehurst. Man, did that give me a spark. I won't horrify you with details of my recovery, but the bottom line is, I played my first round of golf that June.

My first round back, I had to quit after nine holes. I was exhausted. But I was elated because I shot 45. My first prosthetics were very crude, plaster and metal rods. Under the circumstances, it was the best nine holes of my life.

Who was it that was so offended by the term "arthritic grips" that they lobbied to have it changed to "jumbo grips"? I'd like to meet that person and have a discussion about being overly sensitive.

Within ten years, we're going to see a bionic person. I mean someone with complex artificial limbs that receive messages from computer chips implanted in the brain, and which will perform very close to the real thing. Like Darth Vader in *Star Wars*.

I'm the executive director for the National Amputee Golf Association. Our championship this year—our fifty-seventh—will be at Bethpage. We're playing the Red and Green courses because carts are permitted there, and the Black is walking only. More power to Bethpage for that! If the Black were the only course on Long Island, I'd sure want them to allow carts. But there are alternatives, and good ones, which is all the disabled person asks. On the other hand, there's the Old Course at St. Andrews. My dream is to play there someday, but that probably won't happen because carts aren't permitted—except during the British Open, when there are trucks, carts, and other vehicles running all over the property. Come Monday, you can't tell they were ever there. It's not right.

In the mid-'80s I got a letter from an arm amputee in California who had entered a pro-am. At the check-in table the official looked at the artificial hand and said, "What's that?" He was DQ'd before he teed off. After being informed of this, I wrote to the USGA and asked under which rule he was disqualified. P.J. Boatwright responded and referred me to Rule 14-3c on artificial devices. A long discourse ensued between P.J., other members of the USGA rules department, and me. P.J. really was guided by the spirit of the rules.

Not long after, Decision 14-3/15 was modified to say that a person may use an artificial limb even if it assists him in gripping the club. Moreover, the club can have an attachment to help the disabled person grasp it. But the USGA left a loophole, an important "however," which states that if the prosthetic gives a player an undue advantage, then it is not permitted. Fair enough, though I don't think anyone would prefer to play golf with a prosthetic hand,

no matter how good it is. I'm very proud of my involvement in this matter. How many ordinary citizens have lobbied successfully to have a Rule of Golf changed?

Cartpath-only policies stink, don't they? Mowers as big as a dinosaur sail up and down the fairways and across the greens every day. So long as you have the carts scatter—not drive over the same area time and again—they'll do little to no damage in dry conditions. Course operators complain about soil compaction, the spread of disease, and so forth, but these are the same people who put plastic covers over their sofas.

The single-rider cart is the next revolution in golf. There's a model called the SoloRider that is unbelievable—only eight pounds weight per square inch, no more than, say, Ernie Els. They go anywhere, bunkers included, provided there's a flat area to exit and enter.

Disabled people have varying outlooks on life. After the initial period of shock, anger, and denial, most of us just want to get on with living. Others embrace pity that people show for them and turn that pity on themselves. Never show pity for a disabled person. The determined person resents it, and the quitter embraces it. Either way, everyone loses.

One day the phone rings. It's the agent for a famous trick-shot artist, wondering if we'd care to book the fellow to perform for our national championship. There would be a handsome fee, of course. I asked, "Does he hit balls on one leg?" The person said, "He sure does." I asked, "How about with one arm?" Answer: "Certainly." I said, "We have a lot of those folks performing already."

I was in the golf shop one day when a member came in and said, "Bob, will you show me how to hit the ball like you do?"

"I'd be glad to," I said. "Let's go to the range. But on the way we need to stop at my car."

"What for?"

"Because I have a miniature operating room in my trunk, and before you can hit the ball like I do, we first need to remove your legs."

Like I do. That's very key. People have the notion they can be taught to swing like Tiger Woods, but take it from me: Unless you have Tiger's strength, flexibility, speed, and hand-eye coordination, you'll go backward trying to copy him. You're better off going with a method that's compatible with the tools God gave you.

Nobody should play through lightning, but I'm safer than most people. I'm very well-grounded.

Which arm supplies the power to a golf shot? Good question. If I'm a right-handed person and I slap you across the face with a forehand motion, it'll make you dizzy. But if I backhand you, you're going to lose some teeth. So you can argue the backhanded motion is more powerful—certainly it's the power shot in tennis. On the other hand, one of the longest hitters in our association, Quinn Talbot, can hit it 290 using a forehand motion with one arm. The greatest teachers in the world argue about this, and you're asking me?

After Casey Martin was given permission to play out of a cart, the media sought reactions from players. The most memorable I thought was Vijay Singh, who is a pretty tough dude. He said, "I'm glad it passed, because I'm getting older." He sort of smirked, but it pointed up the fact that there are

a ton of baby boomers who will soon be senior citizens. In forty-five years, by 2050, the number of people sixty and older will almost triple. The industry better do something to keep the golfers among them active, something more than the innovation of senior tees. They're going to be your core audience, not the twenty-four-year-olds you see modeling in those equipment advertisements. If the old people quit, the game is not just going to stagnate, it's going to go backward.

Here's how pervasive senior golfers are already: In Florida there are courses that have handicapped parking for golf carts.

Anyone who has walked on stilts will tell you it's harder to stand still than it is to walk. Essentially I'm standing on stilts, which is exhausting mentally because I'm constantly trying to stay balanced. So if you catch me taking a step one way or the other out of the corner of your eye while you're putting, you'll know why.

One NAGA member, Tom Quinn, has made many holes in one. He's a "double AK," meaning he's missing both legs above the knees. He's made two aces sitting in a wheelchair. I envy him. I'd give my right leg to have one ace—but not my right arm.

You see an interesting dynamic at the annual NAGA championship. There are some seriously competitive people there, and some amputees want to beat certain other amputees so badly their game goes to hell. When I first started competing, there was a guy named Dick Bell, a double AK who balanced himself by swinging one of his prosthetics across a sawhorse. He consistently shot in the low 80s, and I could not beat this guy. His disability was more severe than mine, which we both were aware of, and he knew how much I wanted to outplay him. And I could not do it. He'd hit one stiff and grin. "How'd you like that one, Bob?"

My perception—I'm not a pro, but I've taught disabled individuals through our First Swing program for seventeen years—is that strong legs in golf are somewhat over-rated. The golf swing is a rotary, and that comes from the shoulders and hips. The legs move, but only to accommodate the movement of the hips. I've seen double AKs who can hit the ball 270 yards. I don't see how sliding the legs laterally on the down-swing can help anybody.

NAGA offers an annual scholarship grant of a thousand dollars to a deserving amputee. We wish it were more, but we've found that when we conduct a fund-raiser in conjunction with our tournaments, the people who put up the money invariably want the recipient to be a kid from their state. Donors can be funny that way. We're a national organization, but not a real prominent one, so it's hard to do something on a nationwide level. But hey, a thousand bucks is OK. Every little bit helps.

Now I'll ask you a question: What's this thing they call athlete's foot?

Gary Player

It's a mystery that Player, one of the greatest players of all time, isn't regarded as one of the most colorful as well. Surely he is as fiery, tenacious, and emotional as any golfer who ever played, and he did choose as his emblem a dashing black knight. But somehow Player's image isn't quite accurate. He is friendly and outgoing, a master storyteller if ever there was one. Witty, funny, poignant, and dramatic, he held me spellbound for three hours with tales of his native South Africa; his millions of miles traveled; his knowledge of horses, gold mining, and human physiology; his meetings with the legendary Bobby Locke; and his keen perspectives on his arch rivals Jack Nicklaus and Arnold Palmer. Player is still strong, quick, and youthful in both mind and body, and you leave thinking he has an excellent chance of living forever.

○ ○ ○

I've studied golf for almost fifty years now and know a hell of a lot about nothing. Why did Jack Nicklaus, the greatest player in history, change his swing every other week? We're always chopping and changing. Golf is a puzzle without an answer.

I was practicing in a bunker down in Texas and this good old boy with a big hat stopped to watch. The first shot he saw me hit went in the hole. He said, "You got fifty bucks if you knock the next one in." I holed the next one. Then he says, "You got a hundred bucks if you hole the next one." In it went for three in a row. As he peeled off the bills he said, "Boy, I've never seen anyone so lucky in my life." And I shot back, "Well, the harder I practice, the luckier I get." That's where the quote originated.

You can tell a good bunker shot by the sound. From powdery sand, you want a *poof.* From coarser sand, it should sound like you're tearing a linen sheet in half. Strive to make the right sound, and you'll be surprised at how fast you improve.

The worst single food in the world is bacon, because it is pure animal fat. But I have a piece on occasion. I'm not a martyr.

It's true: You are what you eat.

They say Arnold Palmer gave me the 1961 Masters by double bogeying the seventy-second hole. In fact, Arnold wouldn't have had a chance had I not double bogeyed the thirteenth hole and bogeyed the fifteenth. Writers and historians place too much emphasis on the last hole.

The U.S. Amateur is a major championship—for amateurs. I'll leave it at that.

A golfer chokes because he fears being exposed for something less than he really is.

I've flown more than twelve million miles, certainly more than any other golfer, and I think that's more than any human being in history, including pilots. I've spent four years of my life sitting on airplanes.

First I recline the seat. Then I stuff two large pillows where my lower back goes. I place my briefcase under the seat in front of me and put my feet on it. My body describes almost a straight line, like I'm reclining on an ironing board. I drink a bottle of mineral water, put in my earplugs, and in a minute I'm gone. I go to sleep at takeoff and don't wake up until it's time to land.

When you're flying, it helps to be five-foot-seven and 150 pounds.

My dad went to work in the gold mines when he was thirteen. They toiled 12,000 feet below the surface. It was backbreaking, dangerous work. I went to visit him one day, and when he came off the "skip"—the elevator that lowered them into the mine—he immediately sat down. He took off his boot and poured water out of it onto the ground. I asked him where the water came from, and he said, "Son, that's perspiration. It's hot as hell down there."

He told me how men died like flies in those mines. He said a miner's best friend was the rat, because when the rats took off running, it meant a cave-in was imminent. Every day the workers gave the rats bits of their sandwiches as tribute. All this makes me look at my gold Rolex watch differently than most people.

When I was small my mother would take me to tea with her in Johannesburg. "Pull out the chair for Mrs. Wilson," she'd say. "Remember to remove your hat indoors.... Don't reach for the sugar, ask someone to pass it." She was very big on manners.

My mother died of cancer when I was eight years old. The deprivation was hard on me. Many years later, long after I'd reached adulthood, I would wake up in the middle of the night sobbing, dreaming of her and missing her so much. Deep inside, we all want and need our mothers.

I have one barometer to gauge advances in equipment. There's a sprinkler head near the bottom of the tenth fairway at Augusta National that is 182 yards from the center of the green. For years, a really good drive would put me ten yards past the sprinkler head, from where I could avoid a downhill lie. This year, at age sixty-six, playing a tee that is farther back than the old one and hitting to a fairway that has been soaked with rain, I hit it fifteen yards past the sprinkler head. Between the modern ball and titanium drivers, we're hitting the ball fifty yards farther than we did forty years ago.

Tiger or Jack, one six-foot putt, for my life? I'll take Bobby Locke. I've seen them all, and there was never a putter like him. In the hundred or so competitive rounds I played with him, I saw him three-putt just once. He was equally good on Bermuda, bent or bare dirt, and the length of the putt was almost irrelevant. You had to see it to believe it.

My local caddie at the Masters was Eddie McCoy. When I arrived there in 1978, Eddie was upset. "You got to win this tournament, man. I'm in trouble, and I need a new

house." I don't know what kind of trouble Eddie was in, but when I came from seven shots behind to win on Sunday, you've never seen a man as happy as Eddie was. There's a picture taken just after I holed a fifteen-footer on eighteen. In it, you see Eddie flying toward me like Batman, with an expression on his face as though he'd just won the lottery.

One of my heroes is Lee Kwan Yu, the former prime minister of Singapore. He took a nation that was in dire straits and turned it into a vibrant society with a thriving economy. People do not lock their cars or their houses in Singapore. There is no possibility of children being exposed to drugs. Your daughter can walk down the darkest alley without a care in the world. No security guards anywhere, no burglar bars on anything. Now, the penalty for drug trafficking is death. I'm fine with that. The punishment for defacing a thirty-million-dollar building, or a beautiful bridge, with spray paint, is caning. Some people think caning is severe, but I'm for it. It all comes down to what you're willing to pay to live in freedom and peace, without fear.

I've raised thoroughbred horses for thirty-five years. There was one stallion we named Wagga Wagga after a town in Australia. Not all horses are nice, and this one was one mean hombre. A TV film crew asked me to pose with Wagga Wagga. I grabbed his bridle and gave it a sharp jerk to show him who was boss. That's what you do. The camera guy asked me to take a step forward and smile, and like a fool I did. Big mistake.

Just like that, the horse lifted his foreleg and brought it down across my back. His hoof just brushed the nape of my neck. One inch closer, and I would have been para-lyzed or maybe killed. That was a close call.

I took my caddie, Alfred (Rabbit) Dyer, with me to the 1974 British Open. It was the first time a black man had ever caddied in the Championship. I told him, "Make sure you wear your badge here, Rabbit. They're very strict, just like at Augusta or the U.S. Open." Rabbit looked around at the sea of white faces around him and shrugged. "Don't worry about me, boss," he said. "I stick out here like a fly in buttermilk."

There was a weather warning at the Masters one year. Lots of lightning. I was standing on the eleventh tee when they sent vans out on the course to evacuate the players. As I got in, I thought, *My, that's considerate of them.* My next thought was, *Yeah, but what about the 40,000 spectators?*

You don't spend as much time outdoors as I have without having a lightning scare. A bolt hit a tree twenty-five feet away from me once. Knocked me four feet in the air. The bark from this big gum tree was blown eighty yards away and was stuck into a fence. It left a three-foot hole in the ground at the base of the tree. When I hear thunder, I'm gone.

Good vision is underrated. Your eyes influence everything in golf. I wish my eyes were in as good a shape as the rest of my body; it's my only sign of aging. In my business, three yards might as well be a mile.

The best way to break out of a slump is to pretend you're a player whose swing is rhythmic and beautiful. I fell into a terrible slump in 1973, and I recovered just that way. I watched Christy O'Connor at the British Open and stamped his sing-song swing on my mind. For the next few months, I actually pretended I was him. The following April, I won the Masters, then took the British Open in July.

Protesters of South Africa's apartheid policy gave me grief for a couple of years. I didn't believe in apartheid, and I surely wasn't responsible for it, but I was a ripe target. They threw crushed ice in my eyes. Hit me with telephone books at the top of my backswing. Threw balls on the green while I was putting. Burned awful statements into the greens where we were playing. I got death threats at my hotel every day. At the 1969 PGA Championship, a guy screamed just as I stroked a ten-inch putt, and I missed and lost by one. At Merion, during the 1971 U.S. Open, we kept guns in the house where I was staying. I struggled through it, and you know something? It's easier to fight than to run away.

It was a tough two years. But Nelson Mandela, who spent over twenty years in prison, had it a whole lot worse.

I used the same blade putter almost exclusively for more than thirty-five years. Won over a hundred tournaments and the Grand Slam with it. Arnold Palmer and I were walking through a Ginza store in Japan, and I bought it for five dollars. I had it reshafted, regripped, and spray painted black many times, and it almost never failed me. Then one day, a tiny little piece of lead tape I'd placed on the rear of the putter at the outset fell off. I stuck on a new piece of tape, but the putter was never the same. So I put it in a display case for my museum.

Given a choice of being stranded on a desert island with Wagga Wagga or a negative, miserable person, I'll choose the horse.

Samuel L. Jackson

Sam Jackson bounds into the finest restaurant/night spot in Memphis wearing shorts, sneakers, and golf hat on backward. Any apprehension about meeting this great actor is gone in seconds. He is a very youthful fifty-six; when he explains the similarity between his *Star Wars* light saber and his action with a sand wedge, he stands and pirouettes to demonstrate. He orders huge platters of sushi and dives into them with gusto, talking nonstop about golf the whole way, answering every question and asking quite a few himself ("How do you get on at Pine Valley, man?"). Jackson is a willing player; he thunders against sandbaggers at the AT&T Pebble Beach National Pro-Am and his inability to land a top pro, exposes systemic discrimination against blacks in golf as a myth, gives the lowdown on how well he plays when there's cash on the line, and on and on. He is almost self-conscious about belonging to a private club and likes to tee it up at the local muny near his home in L.A. He is the salt of the earth. The ninety minutes I requested stretches to two and a half hours. Sam gets us a private enclave bathed in ultraviolet light, and he stretches out on a sofa as I sit in a chair alongside him, notebook in hand. I feel like a psychiatrist, and it's impossible to probe too deeply.

o o o

My character in *Formula 51* carries his golf clubs throughout the movie. There's one scene where my guy gets into an altercation and uses one of his clubs as a weapon. During rehearsals for this fight scene, I almost killed the stunt man I was going up against. I'd picked a Titleist 3-wood to swing at him, and he was supposed to be just out of reach. Either he got too close or my extension through impact is getting better, because I caught him full force in the head. He dropped like he'd been shot. Blood was everywhere, and my first impression was that I'd killed the guy. Eventually he came back to work, with a lot of stitches in his head. The thought that haunted me was, *What if I'd used an iron?*

During filming of *Star Wars II*, I carried my light saber in my golf bag. I had to practice whenever I could because there were 109 movements to learn. We were in Australia, and I'd whip it out on a tee box when play was slow and go through the moves. The people I played with thought that light saber was very cool. It was about the length of a driver and weighed about the same, too. One of those moves is similar to a golf swing, used to block an overhand blow. The hands lead, like you're playing a knock-down shot, and the block comes high in the follow-through. Apparently the move wasn't good enough. In the final *Star Wars*, Mace Windu gets killed.

If Darth Vader played golf, he'd for sure wear Nike.

What goes around comes around. I was playing with Bernie Mac in Chicago and had just outdriven him by twenty-five yards. I went ahead to my ball instead of hanging back. Mistake. Bernie's second shot was a skull/shank that caught me in the center of the back on the fly. Sent me to my knees, but I realized it was my fault for walking ahead of Bernie. Then again, when a brother has the shanks, there's really no place to hide.

I love showing up at a muny course around L.A., putting my name on the waiting list and then playing with whoever they put me with. That's how I learned to play, looping a public par-three course in Van Nuys all day long. I like the looks of vague recognition I get from the people I'm paired with. A while back, an older couple whispered to each other for a long time until, on the sixth hole, the man said, "You're Coach Carter!"

Can you believe there are still clubs around that don't allow you to wear shorts? It's ninety-seven degrees, and they say you've got to wear long pants. Who's running these places? They always give you the option of buying a pair of pants in the shop for $250, which is ridiculous. When I showed up at Sherwood in shorts and was told they had a pants-only policy until the Fourth of July—they've since changed their policy—I refused to buy a pair. Instead I got into Will Smith's locker and borrowed a pair from him. When I left I put the pants and twenty dollars in Will's locker so he could have them cleaned.

Tiger Woods said in that commercial years ago, "There are still courses in the United States that I am not allowed to play because of the color of my skin." On one hand, I doubt that's literally true, because it's too outrageous for any club to disallow anyone based on race. On the other hand, I believe there are courses that would turn Tiger down for some other reason just to show how powerful they are: *We're the course that turned down Tiger Woods.* It's all about power and exclusivity. They discriminate against everybody.

The day I played with Tiger at St. Andrews, I have to admit I was scared. You can feel the game's history all around you. But I settled down. I shot 78, and I'm pretty proud of that, because people have been known to score worse around there. Tiger gave me some good advice before we teed off. "Stay out of the bunkers," he said.

Tiger's got a temper, but you know who gets even madder? The King: Arnold Palmer. I've played with him several times, including at the Hope, and on practically every hole where he made a bogey, I'd find him on the edge of the green, head down, hissing and growling some language you wouldn't believe. Nobody hears him, but he can color the air blue. If it's OK for the King to get mad, I suppose it's all right if I get mad once in a while.

My Handicap Index is 4.9. It's never been lower, but I had more fun when I was starting out. I felt very little disappointment when I hit bad shots. Today I know what causes my bad shots. Knowledge gives you power, but it also opens the door to frustration and disappointment.

Bill Murray is no fourteen- or fifteen-handicapper. In truth, he's anywhere from a six to an eight, the opposite of the Hollywood guy with a vanity handicap. It's not right that he comes to the AT&T with that kind of number. I like Bill, and it isn't his fault. The tournament officials want to guarantee that he's around on the weekend to boost TV ratings and attendance. He always gets good pros, too. Me, I'm lucky to get a B-level pro. Nice guys, but not players known for lighting it up. It hurts to play your ass off and miss the cut by two shots. It's a conspiracy, man. It ain't fair.

I move it out there pretty good, 270 to 280. Not super long, but definitely longer than average. I was in the group ahead of Corey Pavin at the Hope one year and looked back to where he hit his drive. I was longer. As long as Corey is around, when someone asks if I hit it as far as a tour player, I can honestly say, "Yeah, no problem."

I'm privileged to get to play a lot of outstanding courses. This year I played Winged Foot and then Merion before the U.S. Amateur. I'd heard that it's too short to have a U.S. Open, so I thought I'd cruise around there pretty good. But Merion was maybe the hardest course I've ever played. The rough was brutal, the greens were firm, and those wicker baskets they have instead of flags don't tell you which way the wind is blowing. A couple of weeks later, I played at Glen Abbey outside Toronto, the same course where Tiger hit that beautiful 6-iron from a fairway bunker to beat Grant Waite in the Canadian Open. "What

do you think of the rough?" they asked. "What rough?" I said. "I just came from Merion." The course seemed easy. I shot 81 from the tips.

I tried to re-create that 6-iron Tiger hit. Unfortunately my ball didn't even reach the water, let alone get over it. So I went with a 4-iron, and this time, splash. I was making progress. Eventually I got a club I could reach the green with. I don't mind telling you, it took a 5-wood. That dude is unreal.

I love to sign autographs for kids but insist they say "please." At the AT&T this year, I found myself near the ropes by a large group of kids, all of them waving their programs for me to sign. But I don't hear "please," so I figure it's time to enforce the rules. I announce loudly, so the whole gallery can hear, "What are you supposed to say?" The kids don't answer, they just continue waving the programs. I repeat myself, this time more sternly: "What's the magic word?" Still no answer. I'm ready to walk away when one of the bigger kids, with a look of total frustration on his face, starts mumbling loudly.

Then it hits me: These kids were from a local school for the deaf. They're on their annual field trip. As the adults shot me looks, I started signing and didn't stop until our group fell a hole behind.

Five years ago, a family asked if they could take a picture of me next to their small child. The next year the same family asked me to do it again. We've done this every year for five years now, and I hope they plan to keep going. It's nice to know I look better than a height chart on a doorway.

Given the opportunity, I could have been as successful at golf as I am at acting. I might not have become Tiger Woods, but you'd recognize my name. See, I've always been athletic. I was an only child and became accustomed to doing things alone—golf is a great game for those who enjoy being alone. I've always been able to concentrate. The thing is, it wasn't my destiny. I grew up poor in Tennessee. In our neighborhood we used a Quaker Oats box for a football and a rock wrapped in newspaper for a baseball. There was no way a kid could play golf, even though a golf course was a couple of blocks from my house.

When I took up the game, I fell in love with it immediately and improved quickly. I was almost fifty years old. What if I'd started forty years earlier? Who's to say?

There are some very basic reasons we aren't seeing more minorities excel at this game. Reason number one: Slam dunks and end-zone celebrations are first up on the highlight reels on ESPN. Number two: There are more basketball hoops on urban playgrounds than there are holes in the ground. Number three: Golf balls cost fifty dollars a dozen, and that's just for starters. Number four: It's easier to get a golf scholarship to Jackson State than it is to Oklahoma State, and it's obvious which school is going to produce a better higher education in golf. Number five: The caddie yard is just about gone, and if it's a black caddie yard, that might be a good thing.

I hear of people having these golf dreams that are very frustrating. They keep swinging at the ball and missing, stuff like that. My golf dreams are fantastic. My favorite—and I might have it tonight because I'm talking about it now—is where I play the most incredible individual holes from different courses in succession within the same setting. The eighteenth at Pebble Beach is followed by the tenth at Winged Foot, followed by the fourteenth at Shinnecock. But it's all the same golf course. It's like heaven.

Best golf movie ever: *Dead Solid Perfect.* It got me started playing golf. I can't say much for the rest of them. The irony of the bad golf movie is, the directors usually understand what real golf is about. Ron Shelton, who directed *Tin Cup,* is a good golfer and knowledgeable. But the directors tend to view golf as secondary to the plot, which has to appeal to people who don't play golf. They assume the serious golfers in the audience will forgive the golf stuff and focus on the plot.

My garage looks like an Edwin Watts store. A friend will come over and say, "I need a new driver," and I take him to the garage and he chooses one. I've got fifteen sets of irons ready to go at a moment's notice, and a lot just hanging around. Putters? Around seventy-five or eighty, and the number is going up.

I have a putting green at my home.... No, it's not real grass. How rich do you think I am?

Vijay Singh gave me the best driving key of all time at the Dunhill Links last year: If you're flaring it out to the right, break your wrists earlier and let your right elbow come away from your side.

Stopping at the turn doesn't work for me. I don't like suddenly having a full stomach. I don't like rushing to number ten with my hands full of food, fighting like hell to get my sandwich down before it's my turn to hit. I don't like talking with my mouth full. I don't like having my rhythm broken. I don't like having wet or greasy hands, and looking for something to wipe them off with. I've discovered that with a little discipline, a human being can go four hours without eating something.

Only once did I feel like quitting the game. We played Carnoustie after Jean Van de Velde almost won the British Open there. It was very cold and windy. My feet hurt. The course was hard as hell, and I looked for my ball on probably twelve holes—I hate looking for lost balls. I've never felt so bummed and disillusioned as when I left the course that day. But then it dawned on me that my 85 was four shots better than what Sergio Garcia shot. I realized it was the golf course, not me, that made for such a miserable time. When I got back to the States, I played Spyglass Hill, which is also very difficult, and just sailed around. I felt bad about wanting to quit and promised myself I'd keep things in perspective from then on.

The thing they call "the Zone" in golf has a parallel in acting. Good actors reach moments where a scene happens effortlessly. They get the temperament of the character just right, physically they move easily through their environment and the lines flow from them organically without thinking about it. It's easier for me to reach that place in acting than in golf, because acting is my calling. But I've experienced the Zone in golf frequently enough to recognize the feeling, and I strive to reach it. As we all know, it isn't easy.

I've read about how hard it was to beat Ben Hogan. The old guys talk about how Hogan would give them the silent treatment. If it had been me, I would have fought back. Along the fifteenth hole, I would have hidden his cigarettes.

Tommy Bolt

Tempestuous Tommy "Thunder" Bolt may have been given a gift for shot-making, but the golf gods didn't give him a temperament to match. Bolt was tragedy and high comedy in one roiling, terrible-tempered package. When he wasn't awing galleries with a buttery, powerful swing that produced some of the most imaginative shots ever seen, he was throwing clubs, cussing, insulting officials, chastising spectators, getting suspended, and issuing apologies. But the media loved him, and he was a colorful, cooperative character and an asset to the tour. His career produced several tour triumphs, and a victory in the 1958 U.S. Open. His skittish disposition was complemented by an expressive, tormented face that looked like a clenched fist. When I found Bolt at his home in Cherokee Village, Arkansas, rage had at last given way to inner peace and an almost disarming gentleness.

○ ○ ○

It thrills crowds to see a guy suffer. That's why I threw clubs so often. They love to see golf get the better of someone, and I was only too happy to oblige them. At first I threw clubs because I was angry. After a while it became showmanship, plain and simple. I learned that if you helicopter those dudes by throwing them sideways instead of overhand, the shaft wouldn't break as easy. It's an art, it really is.

For years I was critical of the Senior PGA Tour, especially the way the tour took care of the younger seniors but not the older guys like me. Not long ago I stopped complaining, and the next thing you know I get elected to the World Golf Hall of Fame. It goes to show: You attract more flies with honey than with vinegar.

Arnold Palmer was a good player in any case, but when the crowd got behind him, he became great. It's easier to make birdies for someone else than it is to make them for yourself.

I still play every day. The only difference is, I walk in when my score reaches 80. But Old Tom doesn't walk in very often.

When I won the U.S. Open at Southern Hills in 1958, we still had a thirty-six-hole finish on Saturday. We didn't play on Sunday because that was the Lord's Day, you see. But seven years later, the USGA and television discovered there was a lot of money to be made on the Lord's Day, and that was the end of the thirty-six-hole finish.

I sold newspapers on a street corner when I was about twelve. The first thing I did when I opened my bundle was go to the comic strips and read *Ben Webster—Bound to Win.* The hero, a little kid named Ben Webster, was always overcoming obstacles to win things. Marble-shooting contests, spelling bees, whatever. Maybe because I was poor, Ben became my alter ego. It sounds childish, but on that Saturday at Southern Hills, I was saying to myself, "Bound to win . . . Ben Webster . . . bound to win." It made me feel like I had a little extra something behind me.

The first time I really lost my temper was before I went in the Army. I was working as a carpenter, and in that line of work you're occasionally going to whack your thumb with the hammer. One day I slammed my thumb good, and my helper made the mistake of laughing at me. He stopped laughing when the hammer I was holding missed his head by two inches.

I spent part of World War II as the golf pro at a course in Rome. The course only had sixteen holes because Mussolini, who didn't want his people watching golf, had shut down the two holes that weren't concealed by trees. The Army guys would come there on furlough, and to give them something extra to do, I built a big craps table and ran a dice game. Man, did I get rich. I "faded" those guys—I bet they wouldn't make their point, and most of the time they didn't. I left Italy with a footlocker crammed full of cash. There had to be $50,000 in lira inside that trunk.

Now comes the sad part. On the troop ship home were a bunch of criminals—American soldiers who had spent most of their hitch in the brig. I started another dice game, but these were street guys who knew how to roll dice. Within three days, I'd lost the whole $50,000. When we hit port, my gambling was cured forever.

Some guys might have jumped off a bridge. But money never meant much to me, and I knew I could still make a living as a golf pro or, at the very least, go back to being a carpenter. I just shrugged it off and moved on. *Ben Webster—Bound to Win.*

After I turned seventy, I started setting my goals five years at a time. It worked so well, I wish I'd used the same strategy when I was younger. If you can achieve the short-term stuff, you'll do fine in the long run.

After you turn eighty, you can count on losing ten yards in distance per year.

When the day comes that I hit my pitching wedge and driver the same distance, that's when I'll pack it in.

Here's irony for you: The driver goes the shortest distance when you throw it. The putter flies farthest, followed by the sand wedge.

When you hit an iron shot, you want to take as long a divot as you can. You want it to be long and thin, like a big strip of bacon. You have to apply equal force with both hands to do it. If your divots are short and deep, it's because you're using too much right hand.

You'll see the hole and putt better if you have someone tend the flag on everything outside fifteen feet.

You never stop learning. A couple of years ago I watched Tiger Woods hit a 6-iron two hundred yards out of a fairway bunker and noticed he kept his lower body very quiet. I copied that move, and I probably catch the ball cleaner out of sand than I did fifty years ago.

I wish I could have won the Masters. But I never felt comfortable at Augusta National. I'm always insecure around people who have a lot of money and didn't work for it. The course was perfect for me, but I never played well there, because I resented the people who ran the place. It was my fault, not theirs.

Other than having measles when I was a kid, I've never been sick. I can still read the newspaper without glasses. I can hear my iron shots hit the green. My memory is still good, and I keep my weight down. If I don't make it to one hundred, it will be a total fluke.

Television evangelists disgust me. All of them except Billy Graham. I see the expensive haircuts and three-piece suits and imagine those poor old widows reaching for their purses, and it's all I can do to stop

from coming out of my chair and going right through the TV screen.

By 1957 my playing sort of tailed off, so I decided to take a club-pro job in California. The year I spent behind that counter was the longest year of my life. Treating every member as your boss was one thing, but taking orders from the members' kids was too much for Old Dad. They drove me right back to playing, which was a good thing, because I won the U.S. Open the following June.

My temper was nothing compared to that of J. B., my older brother. When we were teenagers, we pooled our money and bought a set of hickory-shafted irons. One day he had a bad hole, and I watched him go to the side of the green and shatter every one of those clubs against a tree. It made me cry. But I was afraid to say anything to him for fear he'd punch me in the nose.

When I was a kid and poor, I never had shoes that fit. The first date I ever had,

I borrowed a pair of my older brother's shoes. They were a size nine and a half; my foot was a size ten. They hurt my feet so bad I forgot to kiss the girl good night. Later on, I played in tournaments wearing shoes I borrowed from the pro at home. Shoes were always a problem, so when I could finally afford them, I went overboard. At one point I owned seventy pairs of shoes. I can't help but take good care of them. I walk around in them like a cat for fear of wearing them out. The pair I have on right now is thirty years old, but they look new, don't they?

Tour players today must sleep in their hats and shirts. How else could they get that dumpy and wrinkled?

When Bobby Jones won the 1929 U.S. Open in a playoff, the guy he beat was Al Espinosa. It so happens that Al Espinosa shaped the course of my life. When I was thirteen, he showed up at Shreveport [Louisiana] Country Club wearing wingtip golf shoes and the biggest golf bag I've ever seen before or since. Espinosa carried thirty clubs, and me caddying for him was like that scene in *Caddyshack* where the little kid tries to carry Rodney Dangerfield's bag. I could barely lift the damned thing. But between the way he dressed and carried himself and those wingtip shoes, I thought he was the biggest man in the world. That was when I decided to be a golf player.

Before I turned pro, I made a living playing the amateur circuit around Shreveport. As the best player in town, I was able to sell the first-place merchandise prize before the tournament even started. And I'd already have the cash spent before I teed off, which meant I'd have to win to avoid getting in big trouble with the guy who'd bought the prize. That was pressure, boy. But most of the time, Old Dad came through.

For a long time, I had an endorsement contract with a scotch importer. The company reimbursed me for what I drank, and paid me extra besides. It's tough to stay off the sauce when they're paying you to drink it. It's a wonder I didn't become a full-fledged alcoholic.

I never drank so much to where it was a serious problem, but I was drinking more than was good for me. It was my dermatologist, of all people, who convinced me to ease off. I went to see him about my nose, which had gotten big and red. He told me it was because of the scotch. For years after that, I used my nose as an alcohol regulator. It's been in good shape for a long time now.

Mary Lou and I have stayed married for forty-five years because we fight fair and try not to go to bed mad at each other.

I keep hearing that Ben Hogan was a bad putter. I must have missed something, because he was one of the best fast-green putters ever. How else did he win four U.S. Opens? Give him a surface where he didn't have to hit the ball hard, and he could roll that little Jessie like nobody I ever saw.

Never break your driver and putter in the same round.

JoAnne Carner

The grande dame of women's golf has always been utterly without pretense, and that's how I found her at her club in Florida: smoking, joking, having a beer with her cheeseburger, and shooting straight on any topic thrown her way. One of the great women players in history, she invites me out for a quick nine holes when we finish. I partner with her in a gambling game, and she giggles when I hit a shot fat, and struts when she hammers a drive up with my own. I play well, and she whispers, "If you can stick around a couple more days, I think we can make some serious money together." She makes our victims pay up before we leave the final green. As I leave, she tells me a joke: "Mommy, mommy, I'm tired of running around in circles.... Shut up or I'll nail your other foot to the floor." JoAnne is in the top three of the *My Shot* subjects I visited.

o o o

I was standing over a putt in a U.S. Women's Open a few years ago. I glanced down and thought, "My, where did those wrinkles in my arms come from?" I couldn't get the wrinkles out of my mind all day. Now, that's bad concentration. I realized my best days were behind me.

Yeah, I've gone low. I've shot 58—twice. The hell of it is, I can't remember where.

I never made a hole-in-one until my twenty-fifth year of playing. Even now, I've only got six. Only one of them meant much—I won a Mercedes SUV. I had the option of taking the car or cash, and at first I was tempted to take the money. But a friend of mine said, "JoAnne, you've got to take the car. That Mercedes will last forever, and every time

you look at it, you'll remember what you did." That's car's still in my driveway.

Trying to outdrive other long hitters was irresistible to me. Not that it did my game any good. One day I was paired with Mickey Wright, who could also hit it a mile. On the first tee Mickey said, "JoAnne, please, let's not get into a driving contest." But on the fifth hole she let loose and outdrove me by thirty yards. What could I do but try to slug it past her on the next hole?

This went on for several holes, both of us bombing away and hitting the ball all over the golf course. Finally, with both of us out of contention, Mickey suggested we play closest to the pin, a penny a hole. I said, "Why didn't you suggest that in the first place?"

Remember the JCPenney tournament, where a woman teamed with a player from the men's tour? Well, I couldn't keep a partner. My putting drove them nuts. I'd hit the first putt four feet by the hole, and they had to make it coming back. By Sunday night they'd be on the verge of a nervous breakdown. Hubert Green had just gotten over the yips, and he got them back playing with me. John Mahaffey played with me a second time, but only because we were defending champions.

I tried to quit smoking three times. The first time I quit, I was playing in a tournament at Industry Hills in California. I shot 45 on the front nine. I told my caddie to go to the refreshment stand and get some cigarettes, the strongest kind they had. He came back with a pack of Pall Malls, and I shot 32 on the back. For me, smoking and golf go together.

I had the best upbringing in golf imaginable. We played at a little nine-hole course where my brother had a job watering. My brother and sisters, along with the neighborhood kids, played in tensomes after the paying customers were finished for the day. We played a lot of moonlight golf. In Seattle, you sometimes get these incredibly clear skies, and if the full moon is out it's almost like playing in faint sunshine. Playing "down-moon," you could see the flight of the ball from beginning to end. When the moon was in your face, you had to tell by feel whether the ball hooked or sliced. It was wonderful for my game, and about the most fun I ever had.

I've never been a club thrower. It doesn't help.

In 1959, they played the Western Open in Seattle. I met a player there who was very mean. She used intimidation to her advantage, telling players who were away where to stand when she was hitting and so forth. I was only twenty, but she chose the wrong girl when she tried that stuff on me. I'm a nice person, but I'm also one of the most stubborn people on this earth. I ran that woman all over the place, telling her she was away, don't move when I'm swinging, and rolling my eyes at her puny tee shots. I sensed that if I caved in to her, it would hurt my game. And that just wasn't going to happen.

I used to have a three-quarter swing, plenty for a long hitter like me. Gardner Dickinson convinced me to lengthen my backswing, which took a lot of work. But I was glad I did it, because as you age your swing gets shorter, not longer. My swing now is the same length it was when I was thirty.

After I'd won the U.S. Women's Amateur four times, I started taking it too lightly. I'd go a couple of weeks without practicing, just to see if I could win that way. In 1968, I won my fifth Amateur without touching a club beforehand. Don, my husband, was not amused. After I tried the stunt again the next year and got clobbered, he insisted that I start taking the game more seriously. That meant turning pro.

Don passed away three years ago. I don't think I'll get married again. I couldn't go through caring for a sick person again. I haven't even thought about dating. That will change when Sean Connery calls.

Don and I were married for thirty-six years, a long time considering the divorce rate among tour pros. There are more divorces

on the PGA Tour than the LPGA Tour, but being married to a woman tour pro has its challenges. Every husband has overheard someone in the gallery say to a friend, "Boy, wouldn't it be great to have your wife earning a living for you?" Don could cope with that because he was secure financially before he met me. Still, it had to be galling. It takes a special man to handle that.

You may have heard of Beverly Klass, the girl who turned pro at age nine. What I saw of that situation was heartbreaking. Her father was terrible. Beverly was telling me one day about a double bogey she'd made, and we were laughing about it. Her father was standing there, and he slapped her hard across the face. He knocked her down. It was a shocking thing to see. It was so foreign to my experience, I didn't know how to respond. I threatened him verbally, and that was all.

Sometime in the late '70s, thieves broke into the clubhouse at Seekonk Country Club in Massachusetts and stole my beautiful silver trophies. I was sad, but at least they didn't get my gold and silver USGA medals, which were inside a safe in Florida. But then the medals were stolen, too. They were good criminals, and they drilled holes in the safe. The police said the trophies and medals probably were melted down within an hour of being stolen, so there was no chance of getting them back. That's why I have so little sympathy for criminals.

I was the first woman in America to receive a full-ride golf scholarship. I went to Arizona State. I had to work part-time, but I got tuition, room, and board. I'm very proud of that, and we had a great team. The men's team finished fifth in the NCAA Championship one year, and they couldn't beat us.

You look back at the purses women played for in the 1950s and early '60s, and you wonder how they could even afford to eat. Well, a lot of them were world-class poker players. They would look up the biggest card game in town and play for big money. They were good enough at it to make a living. As a rule, women are better poker players than men.

If you want to become a good wedge player, practice hitting balls off blacktop or cement. Blacktop is absolutely unforgiving; you have to hit the ball perfectly. It won't do your sand wedge much good, but most of them have too much bounce anyway.

I'm not big on religion. One of the best things I remember was the time our fam-

ily dog bit the preacher. His name was Rev. Crouch, and we kids called him Grouch because he was so stern and pious. He came to our house one day and told us we were all going to hell for not coming to church more often. The reason we didn't go was because my parents felt bad about not having money to put in the collection plate. The dog, without provocation, trotted over and bit Rev. Crouch good on the leg. He was the only person that dog ever bit. And he never came back to our house.

When men get frustrated or angry, they swear or kick things. Women aren't supposed to behave that way. So we cry.

The tension of playing week in and week out, of being in contention all the time, would build so I could hardly stand it. My way of dealing with it was to watch a very sad movie—something like *The Way We Were.* I would cry uncontrollably, but when the movie was over, the tension would be gone.

As a junior, they called me the Kid from Gravel Pit Road. As an amateur, I was the Great Gundy [JoAnne Gunderson]. In 1976, Sandra Palmer nicknamed me Big Momma, which I like a lot. But the best nickname was the one Don gave me. He called me Curly.

Who hasn't choked? At Rochester in 1982, I was going for my thirty-fifth victory, which would have put me in the Hall of Fame. I had a five-stroke lead after thirty-six holes and got to thinking about the Hall. You can guess what happened next. I lost by seven.

Forget sport psychology. The best cure for choking is old-fashioned anger and disgust.

Chivalry isn't dead, but it's on life support. Won't anybody open a door for me?

You know those teenage boys who wear their pants down low so their underwear is exposed? These are not the individuals who open doors for women.

What's wrong with a sexy image? I'm all for LPGA players promoting themselves and the tour that way. When Jan Stephenson posed on a bed in sexy lingerie, I was all for it. It shows that women athletes can be very attractive, and it sure beat the lumberjack image the tour carried for years. If I had legs like Jan's, I'd pose on a bed, too.

Of course a woman's chest interferes with making a swing. How could it not? The trick is to swing the arms over the bosom, not under. To do that, we have to bend over at the hips a little more to give our arms room to swing. It's not natural. For the record, having breasts is not an advantage.

I have a sick sense of humor. If you stub your toe, I'll laugh. Someone bumping their head is hysterical to me. I've tried not to laugh when people hurt themselves, but I can't do it. It runs against my nature.

Chi Chi Rodriguez

The most valuable commodity in pro golf is the player fans will actually pay money to see. They are fewer in number than we realize, but for more than thirty years Chi Chi was a bona fide "ticket seller," a born entertainer who gave galleries far more than great shotmaking. His sword act was but one piece in his repertoire; he is a wisecracking, animated little fellow who saw golf as theater and worked hard to make people laugh. He also was a true golf genius who won eight times on the PGA Tour and twenty-two events on the Champions Tour. Johnny Miller and many others put Chi Chi in a class by himself when it came to maneuvering the ball, especially with the short irons. When you see up close his tiny hands, gnarled from a childhood bout with sprue, you think it is miraculous he could play at all, let alone become a long hitter despite his frail, 120-pound physique. When you get below Chi Chi's fun and funny surface and revisit his childhood spent in poverty in his native Puerto Rico, the comedian disappears. His face becomes the mournful visage of a sad circus clown, and you understand what a life of overcoming is all about. Chi Chi is a gem, and the content of his 2003 *My Shot* made him one of our best subjects.

○ ○ ○

Do I hold any records? Yeah. I was a bartender at age twelve.

A woman in a van was delivering me and some kids from the Chi Chi Rodriguez Youth Foundation to the golf course from the Orlando airport. When we got in the van, I had a premonition. "When we come to the first intersection, don't be the first car in line," I told her. "A truck full of gravel is going to tip over and hit that first car." She laughed, but I told her it was no laughing matter and insisted she let a car pull in front of us at the intersection.

When the light turned green, a dump truck full of gravel tipped over on that first car. The accident was very violent, and I'm sure someone was killed or injured. I'm clairvoyant. My premonitions of danger have saved me and others many times.

That commercial where Tiger Woods bounces the ball on his club face and hits it is amazing, isn't it? All I could do was run at full speed, bouncing the ball on the clubface as I went along, and bounce the ball on the head of a claw hammer and catch it there, the ball spinning like a top. But Tiger is better than average.

My grandparents on my father's side both lived to be 114. On my mother's side, they both lived to be 100. With genes like that, I think I'll die at 120.

It's a custom in Puerto Rico for the father to have his sons light his cigarettes and hand them to him. That's how I started smoking when I was ten. I smoked three to four packs a day for close to fifty years, then quit. A year later the doctor said I had the lungs of a fifteen-year-old. Genetics are everything. My Uncle Jesus consumed a bottle of rum and five packs of cigarettes a day, and he lived to be 106.

Last week I made a six-foot putt. The crowd applauded. As I walked off the green a lady said, "Chi Chi, you didn't do your sword dance." I said, "Ma'am, that putt was for a double bogey." People must know, to make the monkey dance, you must first give him a banana.

The sword dance is a drama. I am a matador. The hole is a bull. When the ball goes in the hole I've already slain the bull, so the sword fight with the putter isn't necessary except to flaunt my skill. I wipe the blood from the sword with my handkerchief and return the sword to its scabbard. Then I go to the next hole and look for another bull.

I like watching the young guys. All of them except Jim Furyk. I like his swing, but the way he gets over the ball and then backs off—on every shot—drives me crazy. I have to turn the TV off.

My pet peeve is when the commissioner of the PGA Tour walks by our dinner table and says hello to everyone except me.

God gave me fast hands. I was sitting at a bar one time with John Brodie. Out of the corner of his eye he saw my hands flash in the air. "What was that?" he asked. "I'm catching flies," I said. "If you caught a fly out of midair, I'll give you a hundred dollars," John said. I opened both hands and tossed two flies on the table. I said, "Better make that two hundred."

I walked home from the golf course one day with the fifty cents I made caddieing. A man we called Presidio, which in Spanish means "jail," goaded me into playing craps. You're thinking this is going to have a bad ending, but it doesn't. I came home with sixteen dollars—I felt sorry for Presidio and gave two dollars back to him—and my father used that money to put electricity in our house. Many years later, I ran into Presidio. He was wearing a suit. He said, "You made me what I am. My father gave me a terrible beating for losing the grocery money. He sent me to church to ask forgiveness, and today I am a minister."

The best money player I ever saw was Doug Sanders. Here's how good Doug was: In 1964, I was practicing alongside Doug when a spectator called out, "Sanders, you don't hit it as straight as people say you do." Doug turned to the guy and pulled a sheaf of hundred-dollar bills from his money clip. "I'll hit one ball with this driver," he said, "and bet you a thousand dollars my caddie doesn't have to move more than two steps to catch it." The guy says, "You're on." Doug makes the guy show his thousand dollars. Then he hits the ball 255 yards, and the caddie catches it on one hop. His feet don't

move. Doug takes the guy's $1,000 and goes back to practicing like nothing happened.

I don't believe in the death penalty anymore. When was the last time a rich person was executed?

Like all boys in Puerto Rico, I dreamed of becoming a baseball player. My idol was Chi Chi Flores, who was known for his hustle. I ran around the ballpark telling everyone, "I'm Chi Chi Flores, I'm Chi Chi Flores." So they started calling me Chi Chi. I haven't been called Juan since I was twelve years old.

I could have played in the major leagues, by the way. I was a pitcher, and at age eighteen I threw the ball a hundred miles per hour. Faster than Koufax. Ken Still caught Koufax and Drysdale, and he'll tell you, I threw harder. In Puerto Rico I played with Juan Pizarro, Orlando Cepeda, and Roberto Clemente. I wasn't quite as good as Juan Marichal, but I was good. I quit baseball when I joined the Army. You had to choose a sport, and I chose golf, because I figured I could play it longer.

The only difference I see in Tiger's game lately is that he's hitting the wrong club a lot. When I first saw him going long and coming up short, I started watching the situation more closely. You know what? He's not getting along with his caddie. I can see it. The magic between those two guys, the connection that makes a caddie pull the right club every time, is gone.

There wasn't enough to eat in the barrio. We had a dirt floor and no electricity. What I remember most about that was how nice my mother made that floor look. She groomed the dirt till it shined. You didn't want to walk on it, she made it look so nice.

My mother made small fires to cook with. She heated a large can of water once, and my oldest brother accidentally knocked it over. The water went in his ears and burned him everywhere. He died. That was before I was born. But they told me my mother was never the same after that.

We were happy, though. I'd give everything I have now to have what I had then.

For fun we used to swim in the river. A very bad man named Moreno hung out there. He'd take one of us and hold our head under water until our body almost went slack, then he'd lift us out and laugh like hell. He did this to me once, and I told my father. Well, Moreno came into town one day, and my father got his gun. He said, "You had fun with my children, Moreno, and now I am going to have fun with you. Jump, Moreno!" And he fired his gun at Moreno's feet. "Now run, Moreno!" and he fired the gun some more, made Moreno run behind a tree. Then my dad put two bullets into the tree. You've never seen a man so terrified as this Moreno. He never bothered anyone again.

On the first hole of a Southern Open, I hit my drive to the right. I asked my caddie where it went and he said, "That ball is dead." My answer to that was, "It's not as dead as you are. Drop the bag; you're fired." I can't stand being around negative thinkers.

There's all kinds of genius in the world. Ever see a good carpenter hammer nails, one after another, fast, and all of them perfect? That man is a genius—what I call a "muscle genius." The only muscle genius I saw in golf was Sam Snead. And he's the only man I've ever seen who could sit in a chair and touch both elbows on the floor.

One six-foot putt for my life, Tiger or Jack? I'll take David Toms.

All my life I've had the same nightmare. In the dream I can fly, and I land in a cherry tree. A man with a machete stands under the tree and tries to chop my feet off. I hop to a higher branch and then another, until I'm at the top and there's nowhere else to go. Finally I take off and fly low down the road, and a car comes at me. I think I'll tilt my wings and let the car pass under me, but when I try it nothing happens. Just before the car hits me, I wake up sweating. I'd give anything to stop having that dream.

When we were caddies we used to sneak on to the golf course real early. One day I was playing a match with a friend for a nickel. I make a twenty-foot putt, and a toad jumps out of the hole, and the ball, of course, comes out with him. My friend wouldn't count the putt. So when I turned pro, one of my gimmicks was to throw my hat over the hole so the ball wouldn't pop out. The galleries loved it, but some of the other pros complained that I was damaging the hole. Joe Dey asked me to find some other gimmick, so that's when I came up with the sword dance.

David Duval's problem is very simple. Are you listening, David? Let the club dip past parallel at the top. Cock your wrists more. If you've got a strong left-hand grip, the worst thing you can do is shorten your swing.

One day about twenty years ago, Bill Hayes, who started the Chi Chi Rodriguez Youth Foundation with me, rescued a kid who was hiding in the ceiling of a home. His father had abused him so many times he couldn't talk. We took him in, and I worked with him. At first the boy could barely make a sound. He got to where he could stammer, but no words would come out that you could understand. We gave him lots of love and attention, and eventually he was adopted by a millionaire family in Texas. Years later, I asked him to speak at a function for the foundation. He said, "Uncle Chi Chi, what do I tell these people?" I told him he should just speak from his heart. That evening, our boy, dressed in a nice suit, gave the most eloquent speech I've ever heard. I started crying and couldn't stop. The mayor had to hold me. There are a thousand success stories from our foundation, but this one stands out.

Are you listening, David Duval? I just won you five million dollars.

Billy Casper

Billy Casper never exuded that charismatic air of greatness, though great he surely was: fifty-one PGA Tour victories, two U.S. Opens, a Masters, and eight Ryder Cup appearances. In retirement at his home near Provo, Utah, he still is an unassuming presence—a bland, contented face; a slow, fluid walk; and a sense of deliberation in everything he does. For a good spell during the 1960s when the "Big Three" of Palmer, Player, and Nicklaus dominated golf, Casper really was the better player. Only now does he hint that he didn't promote himself as aggressively as he could have, and that the lack of recognition, if not painful, gnaws just a bit. Billy was never known as a good quote, but he opens up as he never did in his prime, giving insight into his genius, recounting his tough time as a youth, and exploring the many rich experiences that came from his being one of the best players of all time.

○ ○ ○

I was sixteen when I watched Ben Hogan play an exhibition in San Diego. He became my hero, and I built my career around his course-management principles. Between that and my own ability, I won fifty-one tournaments on the PGA Tour. I won two U.S. Opens and a Masters, played on eight Ryder Cup teams and captained another. I won the Vardon Trophy five times. If I had never seen Hogan play that exhibition, I might never have amounted to much in golf.

For a time my nickname on tour was the Gorilla. My standard ball flight with the driver was a fade, but it wasn't the type of fade that hit and stopped. It was a low line drive that ran like mad. Bo Wininger thought the ball bounced like a gorilla on the run. The Gorilla...I wish that would have stuck.

In my case, having a big family deflected a lot of the pressure other guys felt. I had a wife and eleven children. That's a lot of mouths to feed, a lot of futures to look after. So I thought about golf in financial terms. I never got caught up in playing for history, seeing how many majors I could win, or rewriting the record books. Those are selfish objectives, and the guy who chokes usually does so because he dwells on what it all means to him. I was only worried about my family. And although I had my share of failures, it was never because I choked.

My family has given me great joy. We've also had our problems. One of our sons, David, is in prison in Nevada and will be there the rest of his life. It's a sickening feeling. In my religion—I'm a Mormon—

there's a saying: "No other success can compensate for failure in the home." Shirley and I have agonized over where we might have gone wrong with David. We gave all of our children the same opportunities, the same guidance, the same amount of attention and love. What happened with our David?

Not long after David was paroled after going to prison for the first time, I had a dream. In it, David was pacing outside our house. I said, "David, come, it'll be all right," and motioned him inside. He looked at me and said, "No, I'm going the other way." It was a vivid dream, the kind that promises something is wrong in real life. Soon after that, David went wild. He committed thirty-five felonies, including armed robberies, got caught after a confrontation with the police, and that was it for him. The day they took David off to prison, he left through a door with a small window. I remember looking through that little window and waving good-bye. Heartbreaking.

We'll never stop loving David, and he'll always be in our prayers. This is not an uplifting story. I don't tell it to sound a warning to others, but to provide some comfort to parents who are having similar difficulties with a child. They should know that it can happen to anyone. So parents shouldn't beat themselves up too badly.

I was at the Ryder Cup last year for a thing called the Captains Challenge. Former Ryder Cup captains stood on the tee of a par 3 and hit shots with the groups that came through. If the amateur hit it inside both captains, he got a new putter and a dozen balls. If he hit it inside one of us, he got a dozen balls. I drew Lanny Wadkins, and he was ruthless. He knifed one shot after another stiff to the hole. The poor amateurs,

their shoulders sagged every time Lanny swung. He couldn't help himself—once a killer, always a killer.

Me, I knifed shot after shot into the water—on purpose. You've got to send a guy to the parking lot with a dozen balls, don't you? The way Lanny was bearing down, you'd think he paid for those balls himself.

Then I watched the Ryder Cup. On Friday I saw something that explained, in a nutshell, why we got beat. Tiger is playing with Phil, and on the eleventh hole, a par 4, Mickelson is in the middle of the fairway and Tiger is in the right fairway bunker. Mickelson is farther away, and to my amazement he hit first, firing right at the flag. Now, why would Phil hit first in that situation? Tiger should have played first, tried to get his ball somewhere on the green from that difficult lie in the sand. If he succeeds, then Phil could, should, go at the flag. It was Golf 101, and they failed.

The first time I played with Hogan we were with Fred Hawkins and Dow Finsterwald. After the round, Mr. Hogan looked at Fred and me. "If you two guys couldn't putt, I'd be buying hot dogs from you on the tenth tee." He was steamed, I think, because his putting was gone by then. The next morning, Mr. Hogan called me over. He looked around to make sure no one was within earshot. Then he whispered, "Billy, tell me: How do you putt?"

If your putting starts to go south, practice hitting short chips from just off the green. When you chip, you pay a lot of attention to making the ball roll perfectly end over end. Practicing that will make your putting stroke come back overnight.

Putting in the dark is the best thing I ever did for my game. On a pitch-black night, when you walk up to the hole just to see where it is, it stamps a very strong image in your mind. You develop a feel for everything: the moisture on the grass, the small change in elevation, the exact distance to the hole, all kinds of things your eyes alone can't tell you. Strangely, that sense spread to the game I played through the air, too. I got more out of those nights on the putting green than I ever did on the practice tee in broad daylight.

A few years back Augusta was lengthened, and Gay Brewer and I shot some big numbers in the first round. The next morning I said to Gay; "If we shoot 42 on the first nine, let's pick up." I don't know why I chose 42. On the ninth hole, I got up and down for par out of the greenside bunker, and Gay three-putted for a bogey. He added up my score, I added up his, and darned if they both didn't add up to 42. We laughed, and we did walk in.

I played golf for twenty-five years before I made a hole in one of any kind. I was on the tour for years before it finally happened. Eventually I made twenty-three, but, boy, that first one was a long time coming. It was the price I paid for not shooting at every flag.

Tommy Bolt was the best ball-striker I ever saw, but his temper was every bit as ferocious as you've heard. I was playing with Tommy in Michigan one year when he flubbed a 4-wood shot from the rough. Then he wheeled and threw the 4-wood as hard as he could, where nobody was standing. A skinny post was sticking out of the ground about thirty yards from Tommy. The club wrapped around that post as neatly as if you were tying a bow. It stuck there, and that, combined with Tommy's rage, made me laugh so hard I couldn't play anymore. A hole would go by, I would picture the club around the post, I'd look over at Tommy; and I'd almost go to my knees. This was more than forty years ago, and when I see Tommy, I still get tears in my eyes.

If your lie is too poor to hit a 4-wood, it's too poor to hit a 4-iron. Go with a 5-iron or less.

At Olympic in '66, Arnold led me by seven with nine holes left. He wanted the U.S. Open scoring record badly. I told Arnold I wanted to finish second—I was a couple of shots ahead of Nicklaus and Tony Lema—and Arnold replied, "I'll do anything I can to help you." I picked up a couple of shots early on the back nine, then two shots on fifteen, two more on sixteen, and another on seventeen. We're tied. On eighteen, Arnold lagged a long putt to within a few feet, leaving himself a tough little putt for par. He was partially in my line and asked what I wanted him to do. "Go ahead, Arnold, you're hot," I said. I wasn't being a smart aleck, it was just my answer. Anyway; he made it, we tied, and I won the next day in a playoff. Some say Arnold was never the same after that defeat, and I have to agree.

I had all kinds of allergy problems with certain meats, and with fruits and vegetables with pesticides. So I turned to bear, caribou, venison, hippopotamus, buffalo, elk, and moose. Tastewise, buffalo and elk are tied for first. Not gamy, and loaded with protein. And very expensive, I might add.

I played in the British Open only four times. The biggest regret of my career. The year I remember best was not 1968, when I almost won at Carnoustie. I remember 1971 better, because if I had missed the cut I would have left immediately for Morocco, where I'd gone many times to stay with my friend King Hassan II. It's a good thing I made the cut, because a coup was attempted the day we would have arrived. People were killed, and friends of the king were fair game. Claude Harmon, Butch's dad, was there, and he was forced to lie on the ground at the golf course for four hours while the insurgents conducted the coup. The king prevailed, and nine days later I went over. Playing well pays off in a lot of ways.

The practice tee is way overrated. On the whole, my advice is to play more and practice less.

I've never felt pressure on the golf course in my life. I felt pressure when I went to Vietnam to entertain the troops, though. One time we were in the back of a Caribou airplane, and the North Vietnamese were waiting for us. They opened up on the plane, and after we landed someone shot a picture of me inspecting the bullet holes in the plane. What scared me was, there were eight barrels of gasoline on board with us. If a bullet had hit one of those barrels, there would have been no use looking for the airplane, the crew, or Billy Casper, because nothing would have been left. Now, that was pressure.

What does hippopotamus taste like? Not surprisingly, it's very watery.

Laura Baugh

As Laura Baugh begins to recount the gritty details of her tumultuous life, you wonder how she emerged with her blue eyes still twinkling, her hair and skin nearly as lustrous as they were in her heyday thirty years ago. Wonder gives way to a feeling of awe that she survived at all. A flinty childhood capped by expectations she wasn't quite prepared to meet. A couple of divorces. An alcohol problem so severe that she bled from her eyes, ears, and even her toenails. A career in which she finished second ten times but never won. Baugh is fine now—fit, sober, and raising her seven children by herself. Beneath her smallish frame, soft features, and sex-kitten countenance lies a survivor with an amazing sense of self-preservation. She smiles ruefully as she tells of the best and worst of it, joking, flirting, growing serious at times, all the while twirling a glass of iced tea and gazing out happily over the golf course that gave her a life both blessed and cursed.

○ ○ ○

I've been around. I played with Colonel Sanders once. *The* Colonel Sanders, the Kentucky Fried Chicken guy. I was only seventeen, and what a weird experience that was. Talking to him was like talking to a Disney character. He looked odd in a golf shirt. I just couldn't get over it. What shocked me was, the Colonel could flat hit it. He told me he loved golf more than chicken.

I'm not a Mrs. because I'm not married anymore. I don't like Ms., and I'm sure as heck not a Miss. I'm just Laura Baugh.

I'm also Fertile Myrtle. I have seven kids. If I were still married, I'd probably have fifteen by now. Bushels of them. If a good

man came along and the setting was right, it would be a blessing to have more.

I finished second ten times on the LPGA Tour. At first I figured the wins would come later, and that I'd do the commercials and stuff to make money and concentrate harder on my golf after I was all set. But I never did win. I started having babies, and when I teed it up between children, I found more ways to get beat than you can imagine.

My six-year-old started first grade a few months ago. For the first time in twenty-one years, I had five hours a day to myself. It was a shocking thing, because for two decades straight I either had a baby in me or on me. So what do I do now? Well, the first day I got my nails done. That was neat. The next day it was like, *What do I do now?* I called a friend, and she told me I needed to get a hobby. That seemed like a good idea. So I decided to take up golf.

After I drop the kids off at school, I go to Perkins for breakfast. Tiger Woods comes in a lot with Mark O'Meara and John Cook. Tiger always walks in with a cell phone to his ear, pretending he's talking so no one will bother him. I've sat there over my coffee and watched him. Man, is he gorgeous or what?

I can't remember not playing golf. I won the National PeeWee five times, the first time when I was three. It was a three-hole tournament, all par 3s. I won my division by, like, thirty-five shots. I was a talented little thing, but remember, this was 1958. There were only three girls in my division.

My dad insisted that I play golf every day. Sometimes it was too much for a little girl. There was a theater in town that had Saturday matinees. The other ten-year-old girls at school got to go to the movies, and I desperately wanted to go with them, but my dad wouldn't let me. "We play golf on Saturdays," he said. I got very angry, but I accepted it, and, in a way, liked it. My whole life, I couldn't play enough golf.

There's this debate as to whether Michelle Wie's parents are doing the right thing, having her compete so much at such a high level at so tender an age. It's a moot point discussing it now, because the cat's already out of the bag. Once you give a kid a taste of something as grandiose as what she's experienced, there is no living way you can roll it back. It would almost be cruel. Did you know Michelle wears a size-eleven

shoe? It's amazing, but it's true. And she'll never wear a size ten again.

My mom and dad divorced when I was eleven. My mom and I moved from Florida to Long Beach, California. She got us into a studio apartment there. Olive Avenue, number 3B. It was in a bad neighborhood. The rent was forty dollars a month. I lived on a diet of popcorn, lemon-chiffon ice milk, and Omega hamburgers. I was cold, hungry, and scared. It was a strange time, because right in the middle of it, at age sixteen, I won the U.S. Women's Amateur. I traveled alone; my dad sent me a standby airline ticket, and I stayed in private housing. There was all this opulence amid the poverty we lived in.

A lot of us kids snuck onto the public courses around town. We'd get kicked off, then sneak right back on. Once we snuck onto the same course three times in one day. For kids who can't afford to play, I have no problem with them sneaking on, so long as they leave the course as they found it. They say there's no such thing as a victimless crime, but I have a hard time feeling sorry for the victim in this case.

We didn't have a TV until I was seventeen. My mom and I only watched TV when we went to my grandparents' house, where I had to watch a lot of *Bonanza*. Since there was no TV, I read all the time. Because of that, I graduated from high school two years early, when I was fifteen, with a 4.0 grade-point average. Stanford offered me a full-ride academic scholarship when I was seventeen—just when I was catching reruns of *Bewitched* and *Gilligan's Island.*

I turned Stanford down. IMG [International Management Group] offered me a thousand dollars to turn pro and go to Japan, all expenses paid. How could I refuse? It seemed like a fortune. Stanford didn't have a golf program, so there would have been no golf. By taking IMG's offer, I figured I'd play professionally for a few years, then quit and go back to school. It didn't work out that way. It never does. You think Tiger Woods is going to go back to college, ever? Please.

My second boyfriend was also my first husband. The marriage lasted a month. He beat me up on our wedding night, and it got worse. Sam Snead, of all people, knew about this guy. "Be careful, Laura," he said. He phoned me a lot to see how I was doing. When the marriage ended, Sam called. "I knew he was bad," he said, "but I couldn't tell you." Sam always looked out for me. He had a softness about him a lot of people didn't know about.

You might want to skip this part. I quit drinking on May 17, 1996, after my "bleed-out." I was drinking so much I started bleeding spontaneously from every place you can imagine. My eyes, fingernails, toenails, ears, mouth, nose, private parts—I was bleeding inside my brain. It was very painful. When this happens, you're dying. The doctors had pretty much given up on me, and people came to the hospital to say good-bye. I was given the last rites. The fact I recovered is extraordinary. I can never drink again, or I'll bleed out again almost immediately and die.

Twenty glasses of wine was nothing to me. Last year I went to a restaurant. A friend asked if I wouldn't like to have just one drink. I looked at the bar for a long time, all the shelves of liquor that were there. I said, "No, thanks. There isn't enough liquor there to satisfy me anyway, so I'll just pass."

One of the beguiling things about drinking is that it can help you play better. Once, in Arizona, there was a rain delay. I went inside and had about six glasses of wine. It was pouring, and I assumed we were finished for the day. Suddenly, the clouds parted, and they called us back out to finish. I thought, *Oh, no.* I hadn't drunk on the course before, and now I've got five holes left. So I go out and birdie those last five holes. That was the worst thing that could have happened to me. At that point I saw alcohol as my friend and savior, when in fact it was the devil in disguise.

Seven kids and an alcoholic mother. It sounds terrible, and it was, but only Chelsea, who was thirteen when I stopped, remembers the nightmare stuff vividly. E.J. was seven when I went into rehab, Haley was six, and Robert was four. They knew something was wrong around their house but didn't know what. In any case, after I came back from Betty Ford, Chelsea was scared of me, and bitter. It lasted several months, but I persisted in trying to reach her. After two and a half years, she said to me one day, "I want you to know that I never respected you when you were drinking. I couldn't talk to you or look up to you. Now it's like you're a different person. I love you, Mom, but more than that, I respect you." You needed a bath towel to soak up my tears.

Thirty years ago, being pretty or sexy was resented, as though it made you something less as an athlete. The attitudes are even more Victorian today. My scorecard was and is blind to the fact I was blond and wore lipstick. Various parties on the LPGA Tour knew it, however, and didn't like it. It's everyone's loss.

I nursed all of my children, which led to a problem when I went back to playing golf. As the round progressed, my breasts would get larger. And larger. Toward the end of the round, I'd begin lactating. At the McDonald's LPGA Championship one year, I was in contention and was approaching the holes that were televised. My blouse was beginning to spot—the pads women wear only help so much—and I started to panic. What could I do? I walked to the water cooler at the back of the sixteenth tee and just drenched myself from my neck to my waist. That solved one problem, although there was still the interference. I never did figure that one out.

I need only two hours' sleep a night. I go to bed at three or four a.m. and get up at six. I listen to the radio, do the laundry, watch the Golf Channel. On Saturdays, I sleep in.

I've never owned an iron. I'm a clothes folder. One of the best ever. A person learns something in thirty-one years of traveling. If you were to see my clothes when they come out of a suitcase, you'd be in awe. No wrinkles, no excuses—that's my motto.

You hear players say, "My goal is to get in contention on Sunday. If I do that enough times, eventually things will go my way." They should know that eventually, things may *not* go their way. How do you think I finished second ten times? If I were in their shoes, I'd play more aggressively, because there's no guarantee someone else will choke.

I'll be honest. I have my dresses and pants dry-cleaned and pressed. But I do fold everything else.

I have empathy for Anna Kournikova. I see a woman who treasures her sport and who worked harder than you can imagine. The problem is, she's pretty and tried to take advantage of that for herself and, not incidentally, her sport. That's the shame of it—the perception that she exploited her looks and never really loved the game or tried seriously to achieve her goals.

I need plastic surgery on my neck and my knees. Too much sun. I'll be careful when I need to get my face done. I don't want to walk around looking like I'm in a constant state of surprise.

You can fall out of love with a person, stop admiring them, and no longer trust them, and still keep a marriage together. It happens every day. But once you lose respect for a person, it's over.

The commercial I made for Ultra Brite toothpaste won a Clio Award. Here's how it goes: A voice in the background says, "Hey, Laura Baugh, how's your love life?" And I say, "What's a love life?"

I'll bet I'm one of the few alcoholics who never smoked or took illegal drugs. It's a good thing, because with my personality, I would have gone overboard with them, too.

At one point I switched to beer. It didn't agree with me—made me so sick I threw up. It was monotonous: drink, throw up, start drinking again immediately, throw up. I emptied the fridge eventually, but beer wasn't my cup of tea.

Charles Schulz was the most impressive person I ever met. He was an extension of his Peanuts cartoons. He was carefree, smart, funny, athletic, and a great family man. I've never met another person who was so happy being in his own skin. For all

his talent, he seemed to admire everyone he met. I always envied the way Charlie looked at life, like it was all too good to be true.

Ladies, to get power you have to move off the ball laterally. Slide your upper body to your right on the backswing and you'll get some extra momentum when you move the other way. That's the key—you have to move back to your left.

At Grand Cypress, we have a rule: If you talk on your cell phone, it's a two-stroke penalty. If you're playing a better-ball match, your team loses the hole. Needless to say, nobody tries to sneak their phone onto the course.

After my divorce, I didn't date for five years. Not once. Last February, my daughter Haley, who was twelve, said, "Mom, I bet you don't have a date for Valentine's Day." That made me decide it was time to get out and talk to big people. I hadn't drunk for seven years, the baggage from my marriage was behind me, and I could tell the kids could probably use a break from me. So I started going out again last year, and it's been fun, though a little like taking up golf again. It's awkward at first, but then it comes back to you, like riding a bike.

I'm not quick to admit it, but I can install doors, rebuild a drain field, do some plumbing, and get the car fixed without getting ripped off. A single mother learns how to do these things.

If you play badly but get something out of the round—like learning you can't hit a 4-iron out of a divot—then it was a good day. Take what you can, and be happy. If you judge the round solely by what you shot,

you're going to be disappointed, because most of the time that number is higher than you thought it would be.

Don't lie to me. Not even little white lies. Tell me you like the color of my dress even if you hate the design. I'll get the hint.

Men are more vulnerable than women. They're more susceptible to being manipulated. I've known so many successful men who were brilliant intellectually or in business who've been taken for a ride by a woman. Women do have their crosses to bear, but when it comes to love, women generally fare better than men.

Because I'm forty-eight, there's a perception that the field of available men is narrow for me. In fact, it's incredibly wide. Someone who looks old enough to be my father would obviously be too old anyway, and a guy who looks old enough to be my son would be too young. The age span in between is extremely generous. I know one thing: There's no rush.

What would a man love most about me? My kids. They're my greatest asset, my biggest drawing card. He won't believe how wonderful they are. After he recovers from what it costs to take all eight of us out to the movies, he'll realize that the package deal—and it is a package deal—was more than worth the price of admission.

I always wanted to be a children's dentist. I knew I'd be making a difference. And that I could play golf on Wednesday afternoons.

I found that I played just as well wearing lipstick as I did without it. There's no downside to trying to look as attractive as you can.

Of course there are gay women on the LPGA Tour. The percentage is probably higher there than the percentage of gay women in theater. On the other hand, the percentage of gay women in golf probably is lower than that of gay men in theater. What I'm saying is, there are gay people in every walk of life. You know that. Let's move on.

People assume that I somehow know more than I did twenty years ago. In some ways that's true. But my math is worse, and my memory stinks.

Men with gray hair look great, whereas women are told they have "character." But the right shade of gray can make a woman look stunning. Color the hair shining silver, and an older woman can look beautiful in a way a young girl can't.

The secret to wearing mascara in hot, humid weather: First you apply a thin layer of mascara. Then apply a thin layer of baby powder. Another thin layer of mascara and you're set.

They make golf gloves to accommodate women with long nails, but they aren't always available. So do this: Take a razor blade or scissors, and sever a few of the stitches on the seam at the tip of each finger so your nails pop through. Works perfectly.

People see other people do shameful things and say, "I'd never do that under any circumstances." My answer to that is, "You might be surprised."

Lee Trevino

During the early 1990s I met with Lee Trevino several times to help him write instruction articles for *Golf Digest*. Usually we worked at Wethersfield Country Club in Connecticut, where his mother-in-law owned a home in the middle of the golf course. The first few times, when we finished up it was good-bye and over-and-out—Lee would disappear into the house and that would be it. Trevino was notoriously difficult to bond with, and I accepted our relationship for what it was. On the fourth occasion I guess he decided we were now friends. He invited me inside, handed me a cold drink, and gave me a tour of his workshop. For the *My Shot* interview in 2002, Lee invited me inside again and was chatty even for Lee, talking away for three hours at the kitchen table while Claudia did some preliminary work on Thanksgiving dinner. The game never had a better promoter than Lee, and few players were greater—he won two U.S. Opens, two British Opens, a pair of PGA Championships, and twenty-nine PGA Tour wins. As his Boswell for those instruction articles and this *My Shot*, I can attest that a writer never had a more loquacious subject than Trevino.

o o o

People tell me I look healthy for being sixty-two. I don't let it go to my head. I've been to too many wakes where people look in the casket and say, "Don't he look great?"

Only bad golfers are lucky. They're the ones bouncing balls off trees, curbs, turtles, and cars. Good golfers have bad luck. When you hit the ball straight, a funny bounce is bound to be unlucky.

I keep a lot of my opinions to myself. My grandfather, who was a gravedigger, told me one day, "Son, the next time you go by the cemetery, remember that a third of the people are in there because they got into other people's business."

I believe in reincarnation. In my last life I was a peasant. Next time around, I'd like to be an eagle. Who hasn't dreamed they could fly? They're a protected species, too.

Green synthetic practice mats are the worst thing for your golf game that I know of. You can hit six inches behind the ball and not even know it, because the ball still gets airborne. Practice nets are awful, too. Swing a weighted club instead.

People ask me who's better, Tiger or Jack. It's close, but if they played one eighteen-hole round, both men in their primes, I'd have to take Jack. He was longer than Tiger, a better putter, and he'd game-plan Tiger to death. Nicklaus at his best always found a way to win.

The first sign a guy is choking is when he looks up too early on a putt. He'll decelerate and miss to the right. When your opponent does that, you've got him.

Don't ask me to shake your hand when I'm in a restaurant having dinner. No offense, but I don't know where your hand has been.

If your concentration is getting bad, take up bass fishing. It will really improve your ability to focus. If you aren't ready when that fish hits, you can't set the hook.

Show me a golfer who doesn't have a mean streak, and I'll show you a weak competitor.

To be the best at anything, you have to be a little selfish. Selfishness is the reason I didn't know my first four children. I could have been a better dad, but I would have been an average golfer.

If I'd never discovered golf, I wouldn't have minded being a bulldozer driver. I like feeling that power under me. A good 'dozer man can move dirt the way a sculptor shapes clay. Nobody saves the golf course builder more money.

I just got twenty-eight teeth crowned. I had the dentist grind them all down in one nine-and-a-half-hour appointment. When he put the crowns on, I did it without Novocain. I have a high pain threshold.

Golfwise, I did it all by myself. I'm not indebted to anybody for the game I've got. That's my single biggest source of satisfaction.

I went flat broke in 1977. It didn't bother me a bit. If you've been poor once, being poor again is no big thing. You just look at it as a challenge.

If you think a guy is trying to hustle you, just make two bets. One match, one medal. It's real hard to lose both.

One day in 1984 my wife, Claudia, told me, "The government gets a third and we can spend a third, but we need to save a third." That's the smartest advice anyone ever gave me. We're rich now.

You can't go through life not trusting any-one. Sooner or later you have to put your faith in someone. And no matter how well you judge character, it takes luck to choose the right person.

No one has explained to my satisfaction why a one-way airline ticket can cost more than one going round trip.

I've been hit by lightning, had back opera-tions, torn ligaments in my thumb, and a million other things. But I'm still playing, because I have the best physical therapist in the world. She's sixty years old, is about six-foot-five and just beats the hell out of me. Her thumbs are like hammers. Every week for two hours, two hundred dollars a session. Longevity comes with a price.

Chuck Rubin signed on as my agent in 1989. He said, "I'll only do it if you have me au-dited once a year, because I don't want any question in your mind about where your money is." Sweetest words I ever heard.

Unless you're a pastor, priest, minister, or rabbi, you have no business pushing your religion on somebody else.

If you ever get in a fistfight and you're bigger than the other guy, stay in close and try to get him on the ground. If you're smaller, stay away. Regardless of your size, think twice before throwing the first punch, because you're making a big commitment.

Speaking of fistfights, the last one I had was in 1975 with the mayor of El Paso. We had bet two hundred dollars on who had won the last El Paso Open, held in 1959. He guessed it was one of the Hebert brothers, but I knew it was Marty Furgol. When I came to collect, there was a TV crew waiting, and here came the mayor with two huge bags full of pennies, a hundred dollars' worth. He poured one bag of pennies over my head, which I didn't think was one bit funny. I warned him not to pour the other bag over my head, but he just laughed and started to pour anyway. So I cold-cocked him. When they showed me punching out the mayor on TV, I got a lot of phone calls, all of them congratulating me. People didn't like that mayor.

Tom Jones is the best damned stage performer of all time. I only wish he would have sung more ballads.

I don't mind signing autographs. But I won't sign skin, gum wrappers, towels, or napkins.

I claimed to have quit smoking many years ago, when in fact I'd still sneak one now and again. Then, in 1995, my daughter Olivia, who was six at the time, caught me lighting up. "Why are you smoking, Daddy? That's bad for you." I thought she was

gonna cry. That was my last smoke. Some people use the patch; I used my own guilt.

There are people who think Bill Murray is hilarious. Frankly, I don't get it. His movies are okay, but as a comedian, give me Alan King any day.

I think they should change the rules so you can lift, clean, and place your ball, but only in your own fairway. Who hasn't found their ball in a divot in the middle of a fairway and thought the same thing?

I can look a guy in the eye and tell how tough he is, whether he's a fighter or not. You know who's a fighter? Our president, George Bush. He is one tough cookie who will lock horns with you in a second. He likes a good fight, and right now I'm glad he's in charge.

My advice to architects: Before you build a course with deep bunkers, railroad ties, forced carries, and water everywhere, just remember that no Donald Ross course has ever gone Chapter 11.

Unless you're in prison, you have to agree that life in America is better than it's ever been.

If I were a judge, I'd send every gang member into the Marine Corps for two years. I guarantee most of them will come out ready to contribute to society.

I can't work a computer. I'm afraid I'd like it too much. My day is crammed full as it is.

Sure, I believe in ghosts. I know there are ghosts at St. Andrews. When you walk across the Swilcan Bridge you can almost see them, they're so close. The Morrises, the Auchterlonies, I'm certain they're all flying around out there.

Practicing all the time helps my confidence more than it does my swing. Knowing you've paid a price gives you a big advantage.

It's hard for me to visit sick kids in hospitals. I don't do it anymore, because it tears me up too much. But I do other things. After I made a hole in one worth a million dollars last year, I gave $500,000 of it to St. Jude Children's Hospital.

I've met a lot of celebrities, but I've never been so awed by another person that I couldn't be myself. That would change if I got to meet the Pope.

I have a confession to make. In 1984 I was using one of those early metal drivers I'm pretty sure was nonconforming. Other guys used them, but the drivers didn't work for them, because they kept caving in the faces. Not me. I didn't hit the ball hard enough to hurt the clubface. And I did get a little extra distance with it.

It's no secret I can be very snappish with people. I always end up regretting it. Last year in Utah, a little boy asked me to sign his golf ball and I told him no. I couldn't

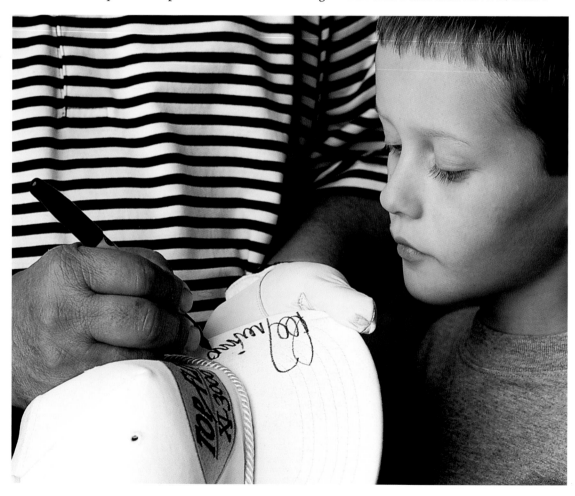

eat dinner that night and slept for about an hour. The next morning, a security guard helped me find the boy. I gave him a signed ball, a glove, and a hat. The kid was ecstatic, his dad thanked me, and as I walked away I swore I'd try to be nicer to people. And I am getting better at it.

I felt a fly land on my chin. When I went to brush it off there was no fly. It was drool. You know you're close to retirement when you can't swallow your own saliva.

Golf programs for inner-city kids don't work. After they bus the kids out of the ghetto and let them hit balls for a few hours, they bus them right back to the ghetto. I've thought about this for thirty years and still don't know the answer. I'm not sure there is one.

If I don't come back as an eagle, I'm coming back as a traffic cop. And I'm giving a ticket to every jackass on a motorcycle who passes cars between lanes.

I know people in Dallas. Trust me, Oswald didn't act alone.

Evel Knievel

Celebrities like to frequent the Alize at the Palms restaurant in Las Vegas, and the sight of them is so common that they rarely cause a stir. But as I follow Evel Knievel to our table on a weekday evening, diners nudge each other and point him out. Men whisper to their wives and several call out his name. Say what you will about Evel Knievel, he has etched a special, enduring place in American culture. His adventures in golf were almost as harrowing as his motorcycle jumps. Always the daredevil, he gambled excessively with hustlers and still refuses to play unless there's "a little something" at stake. He won and lost fortunes that way. He teed it up with celebrities, played blackjack with Arnold Palmer watching, and even teed it up while serving time in jail for assault. Evel, lugging an oxygen tank, was philosophical, brutally honest, and unrepentant. He grew angry talking about cheaters, laughed at the funny things he remembered, and became emotional talking about the game itself. Evel played the interview straight up, and when I sent him the galley proof for his review, he didn't change a word.

o o o

I'd make a jump on a motorcycle before I'd jump with a golf cart again. In the mid-'70s I played a lot of golf at Rivermont in Alpharetta, Georgia. The seventeenth hole there is a par 3 that's steeply downhill. The path has a series of hairpin turns, and if you ignore them you'll just keep going over a huge ledge. The guys I hung out with down there pointed out that if you gathered enough speed you could go over the cliff and land where the path resumes farther down the hill. For days they dared me to make the jump, and when I came to the hole in a foul mood one afternoon—I wasn't playing well—I just went for it. Halfway down the hill I realized I'd made

a mistake. You have no idea how unstable a three-wheel golf cart is when it becomes airborne. By the grace of God I made a perfect three-point landing, but the tires were like basketballs, and the cart bounced like an SOB. When I got the thing stopped down near the green, I immediately got a royal chewing out from my wife. I couldn't blame her. She'd been in the passenger seat the whole time.

Carts are unstable on the ground, too. Some years ago my son Kelly had just finished playing the front nine with friends at a course in San Diego. The starter asked if a single, a guy from Japan, could join them.

Kelly said sure, and the guy strapped his bag on the cart and jumped in. It was the last thing that poor guy ever did. As Kelly was rounding a curve, the guy fell out as he was reaching for a pack of cigarettes, hitting his head. He was killed instantly. It was a traumatic thing for Kelly. He's a good boy, a plus-one handicapper and winner of the Las Vegas city amateur championship. But he was grilled for two days before the police let him go. He very nearly quit playing golf because of it. He still plays, but he's awfully nervous about driving the cart.

My grandpa got me a set of Wilson clubs, Sam Snead models, when I was twelve. Many years later, when I'd become well known, I got to know Sam, and we played a lot of golf together. He'd give me two shots a side, jump in his cart with that big dog of his, and off we'd go. I never did beat Sam. We tied a few times, and I took pride in outdriving him, but you could forget about taking money from that man. Then he'd rub it in. When I wrote the check, he insisted that I write "golf lessons" in the memo section, so he could write it off.

I learned one thing from jumping motorcycles that was of great value on the golf course, the putting green especially: Whatever you do, don't come up short.

You'd think a guy who has broken thirty-five bones in his body would have a high pain threshold, but mine is pretty low. I got hit in the shin with a golf ball once, and it almost brought tears to my eyes. I've had broken bones that didn't hurt as bad.

I was playing twenty-one at the Aladdin in Las Vegas, betting $10,000 a hand. Arnold Palmer and Winnie are standing right behind me, watching. And I'm losing. The dealer is pulling twenty every time, and although I'm pulling my share of twenties, too, I can't win a hand, and I'm losing a lot of money. And I'm getting really angry. The next hand he deals me a twenty, and he's got a face card showing. I'm certain he has twenty, and I just can't bear trying again. So I ask for a hit. The dealer freaks out, shuts the table down and screams for Ash Resnick, who runs the casino. Ash comes along and is told I want to hit twenty. He looks at me for a long time and then says, "Give the kid a hit." The dealer gives me an ace, and when I turn around, Arnold's eyes are this big and Winnie looks like she's going to be sick. "I know what pressure is," Arnold said, "but you're too much."

Arnold gave me a great lesson once. We were at Bay Hill, and I suggested that we play for some cash. He put his arm around me and said, "Evel, I've got a lot of money, and I don't need any of yours. On the other hand, I don't want you to have any of mine." That taught me something about gambling with friends. Keep it friendly.

I was making a jump in Dallas one year and hooked up with Amarillo Slim. Now there's a man who knows how to gamble. Slim bet me that I couldn't break 80 at Preston Trail the next day. I was a good six-handicapper and had played the course, so I knew I had a good shot, and I bet him $10,000 I could do it. When I woke up the next morning, there was three inches of snow on the ground. There was no getting out of the bet; Slim had been careful to stipulate "tomorrow," with no questions asked. I paid up, and had no problem with it whatsoever. If you're going to be sucker, be a quiet one. Nothing's worse than a guy who loses fair and square and then whines about it.

One of Slim's favorite tricks was to bet that two of any twenty-five people chosen at random would have the same birthday. He always won that bet—the math was huge in his favor.

We were playing a big-money game at Las Vegas Country Club. My partner was Jay Sarno, the fellow who built Caesars Palace. One of the guys we were playing against was a terrible cheater, so I knew we had to keep an eye on him. One of our side bets was that nobody could reach a certain par 5 in two. After we hit our drives on this par 5, I had my back turned to him when he hit his second shot. He hit the green and started yelling that he'd won the bet.

What he didn't know was, I had a Zebra putter, the kind with the shiny steel plate on the sole. I'd watched him through the soleplate, which was like a mirror. I went straight over and gave the guy a push. Under his foot was a tee. Well, I pulled a .44 magnum from my bag and chased that guy around the course until I cornered him between some condos. He was on his knees begging me not to kill him.

To this day I don't know what stopped me from shooting him. The sheriff was called out, and he let me go, because he knew the kind of man this guy was. The sheriff told me I'd be best off not playing

golf for money in Las Vegas, because that town has the worst cheaters in the world.

I figure I've lost close to half a million dollars on the golf course, most of the time to cheaters. See, the honest games are small games. Big money is what attracts the thieves, and it was well known I played for big money. In hindsight, the solution would have been to bring a lie detector, hook the people up, and start counting backward from twenty. When you reach the number that doesn't set off the lie detector, that's their handicap.

I spent a short time in Mira Loma prison for hurting a guy with a baseball bat. He'd written some stuff in an unauthorized biography about me that was completely untrue. To make life in the joint a little easier, a friend of mine dropped off my big Sam Snead golf bag and bright yellow shoes, which were given to me by Doug Sanders. My friend set them at the side of the freeway near the field where I worked, and a guard retrieved them for me. I hit balls for several days, striping irons and drivers across this field. People driving by would honk, wave, and shout at me. It must have been a strange sight, Evel Knievel playing golf in an orange prison jumpsuit and bright yellow golf shoes. Well, one of the passersby reported me to the authorities, outraged that I was treating the prison like a country club. I was transferred to the Los Angeles County Jail, where I was put in a cell next to Charles Manson, who used to give me the evil eye, but he didn't scare me one bit. That was a miserable place. I regretted hitting balls in that field. I should have hung out at the putting green next to the field that was built for the prison officers. I never would have gotten in trouble, and frankly, my short game really needed work.

Golf brings out the best in a good man and the worst in a bad man.

When you get injured, it's important to get back on your feet as soon as possible. After I broke my back and leg in a jump in San Francisco in 1972, I recovered by playing golf. I went up to Winged Foot in New York, where Claude Harmon was the pro. I was still on crutches and really couldn't hit my driver, but my irons were fine. I was in a mood to gamble, and Doug Sanders was around. Doug would play for anything. We went at it, with the stipulation that I didn't have to hit a drive. Claude would put my ball down at the 150-yard marker, and I'd play the hole from there, lying one. Well, I lost $40,000. Doug left to play in a tournament upstate, but he missed the cut and came back to Winged Foot for more action. Claude was the best sand player I ever saw, and a great teacher. He gave me a bunker lesson while Doug was gone, and when Doug came back, I won $50,000—the amount I lost and a bit more. I was always grateful to Claude for that lesson.

If you don't want to play for anything, I won't play with you. Gambling is part of being a man. If you don't have guts enough to play for something, I question your manliness. You should just stay in your element, and I'll stay in mine.

Golf was spiritual for me. I loved being around the trees, the sun, the water, and fresh air. It was like being next to God. But that changed on a day two years ago when I played at my home course, Butte Country Club in Montana. I got into a money game with four other guys. I knew three of them, and the fourth, they said, carried a twelve-handicap. The stranger birdied the first hole. On the second hole I caught him stepping behind his ball in the rough and claimed the hole. He parred the third hole, and on the fourth, he hit his approach one inch from the hole. At that point I really smelled a rat. I drove my cart over to the four guys. "Gentlemen, for all intents and purposes, this game is over. If you think you have money coming and want to discuss it, I'll be waiting in the parking lot with a .44 magnum." They didn't show up, of course. I learned later that all four men had set the game up in a bar the night before we played. That day broke my spirit, to realize that friends would try to take advantage of friends like that. I'm just now beginning to find the urge to play again. When I do, it will be with friends. And we won't bet thousands of dollars, we'll play to see who buys dinner.

You get the idea some players would rather take a bullet than sign autographs. They need to think about when they were kids and had heroes, and how they would have felt if their hero had told them, "Go to hell, kid; I ain't got time." They need a refresher course on the fact that, whether you're jumping motorcycles, playing golf, or juggling in a circus, it's all about the fans.

Given a choice between being a pro golfer and doing what I did for a living, I'll take what I did. It's a good feeling, earning your own money, playing for your own stakes. Pros play for someone else's money. It's almost unbelievable the way they can choke when they literally have nothing to lose.

No doubt about it, I've choked on the golf course. But I'll tell you, as great as the pressure was, it was nothing compared to some of those jumps I made. When your life is at stake, you find out what real choking is. Eventually I lost my nerve to jump. Even if I were physically able to get back on my motorcycle and jump, I couldn't do it. Your nervous system can only take so much, and mine is shot to hell.

As for golf, I'm ready to play again. I have a bad pulmonary disease, and there's no cure. The doctors have given me three years. My lungs are hardening, and the damned part of that is, I never smoked a cigarette in my life. But I'm ready. I'll bring the oxygen tank, and we'll play for a thousand. You up to it?

Jackie Burke

He is the grand sage of American golf, his observations on the game a dizzying blend of humor, wisdom, encouragement, admonishments, and profundities. Burke won two majors, played on five Ryder Cup teams, and won a bunch of tour tournaments, including the 1956 Masters and PGA Championship, but his greatest accomplishment (in his mind anyway) was founding Champions Golf Club in Houston. Champions has become a template for what modern-day clubs should be, and Burke's doings there helped land him a spot in the Hall of Fame and also the Bob Jones Award, a prestigious honor given by the USGA. Burke is still at Champions, thundering away into his eighties and keeping his profile high enough that he was selected to cocaptain the 2004 U.S. Ryder Cup team. His musings in this *My Shot* inspired him to write *It's Only a Game*, published in 2006.

o o o

When I taught at Metropolis Country Club in New York, there was a fellow who shanked chip shots, nothing else. The man smoked a pipe, and after a lot of thought I began placing his best pipe just outside his ball. He was terrified of hitting the pipe with the toe of the club, you see, and I cured him quick. I was telling this story in Houston not long ago, and a member overheard it and disappeared. He came back an hour later and placed his pipe, which was shattered to bits, in front of me. "Your tip doesn't work for long irons," he said.

Live your life so that when you die, you fill up the church. A big funeral says something about how much you were loved, or at least respected. These people who get to the church by way of the electric chair don't get much of a turnout. They have to rent the pallbearers.

Stomping around in search of a sprinkler head that has "162" stamped on it is a complete waste of time. Before they invented the 150-yard marker, we used a formula that worked better than numbers. Determine what club you'd need to use—with a thousand dollars riding on it—to fly the ball over the green. You have to be honest with yourself. There's a thousand dollars at stake, so you better not underclub. If that club is a 6-iron, simply take one club less— the 7-iron—and hit it firmly or softly, depending on whether the hole is front, middle, or back. The formula never fails. It also teaches you feel, touch, and a sense for wind and elevation. One more thing: It'll cut half an hour off your round.

When I won the 1956 Masters, I had a downhill putt on the seventeenth hole that was lightning quick, and it was made even faster because the forty-mile-per-hour wind had blown sand out onto the green. I just touched that putt, and I immediately thought, *Oh no, I didn't get it halfway there.* Then the wind grabbed that thing and kept blowing it down the hill, until it plunked dead in the middle of the hole. It was a miracle, the best break of my career. You better believe wind affects putts. A golf ball weighs 1.62 ounces. Can a twenty-mile-per-hour wind affect that ball as it rolls? You tell me.

When I look down the fairway from the tee and want to play a fade, I see a huge wall on the left edge of the fairway. I see a jai-alai court, where the ball will bounce off the wall and back into play if I miss the fairway. That gives me mental freedom and the ability to swing with a bit of recklessness, which is necessary to be a good driver of the ball. Take that wall down, and you get tense and start steering the ball short and crooked. Let it go, man! Freewheel it!

Hang the Mona Lisa in a country club boardroom, and sooner or later an incoming president will lobby to have her hair repainted.

When you're playing as a guest, offer to pay for your caddie. And don't ask your host how much you should pay him. Be generous. Think of what you paid a caddie the last time you used one, and give him twenty dollars over that amount. For God's sake, help the guy. I've never seen a caddie leave the parking lot in a Cadillac.

Sometimes winning is easy. In 1958, Ken Venturi and I toured Japan. The morning after we landed, they took us out to our first "exhibition," which happened to be the Japanese Open, their national championship. Ken played great. He finished the last round thinking he'd won comfortably and sank himself in one of those huge, luxurious tubs, with enough sake to drown Godzilla. But playing a couple of hours behind Venturi, I got hot and tied him. I found Ken in that tub of hot water and told him to get his butt out of there and onto the first tee, that we were in a playoff. A few minutes later, they got Ken to the first tee. Like I said, sometimes winning is easy.

To succeed at golf, you have to master the art of not being embarrassed. It's incredibly hard to erase thoughts of how you're going to be perceived by others, and the challenge never ceases. You think Arnold Palmer doesn't feel embarrassed when he yips a four-foot putt in front of a big gallery? He mastered the art of not being embarrassed years ago, and now he's learning it again.

I was raised in a good house. The worst luck someone can have is coming up in a bad house. It can be too much to overcome. Remember that when you look around.

Can you guess the sport? You check in and they hand you a scorecard. They may ask for your credit card. You put on special shoes, then play the game without knowing or meeting the people playing all around you. You get in the car and leave, thinking maybe you'll do this again someday, and maybe not. If you guessed bowling—or resort-course golf—hop to the head of the class.

Everybody wants to retire early. Well, I've seen early retirement, and it's not pretty.

These fifty-year-old guys hang out at the club constantly, because they have nowhere else to go. They get sick of golf; you never see them smiling when they're coming up eighteen. Don't retire. Leisure time is dangerous. You might wind up inside a bottle of bourbon. You are put on this earth to produce, so get with it.

These high-end public courses can't possibly work. A family of four for four hundred dollars? When it's over, you look in your wallet and think, I hope the kids don't ask if we can do this again tomorrow.

The First Tee program may or may not succeed. Why it became necessary to build these facilities for kids is a black mark on the record of all local clubs and courses. If local clubs made an effort to include young people rather than exclude them, the First Tee wouldn't require the huge amounts of money and effort they're putting out. What if every club in America brought kids in twice a year and did all they could to make them feel welcome? The kids would aspire to be a part of that club. They'd study and work hard so the club could be attainable one day.

The game is growing, all right—just look at the stomach of your basic country club member. The emphasis on food in clubs is just unbelievable. The chef is praised or vilified more than the head pro.

To get into Champions, your handicap has to be fifteen or less. I don't care how much money someone has, what race, sex, or religion they are, none of that stuff. All I want are people who have invested a lot of hours in the game. A respectable handicap usually reflects that. I have nothing against high handicappers, but I don't want them in the majority. It doesn't make a lot of sense filling a yacht club with people who can't sail a boat.

Don't get me wrong: I believe that if you lock a hundred bulldogs inside a yard, you're going to wind up with some funny-looking bulldogs. I believe in diversity. I don't lock the gates. I want all kinds of people from all walks of life, with one thing in common: a sincere appreciation for golf and what it should be. I liken us to Stanford University, or Yale or Harvard. They don't accept D students academically, and we don't accept people with a D average in golf.

At the top of the backswing, imagine your right hand is filled with seeds. You want to spread those seeds on the ground evenly over as wide a distance as you can. Through impact, you can only disperse those seeds properly if you maintain an angle in your tight wrist. If you flip your right wrist too soon, those seeds will fly up in your face or go anywhere but across the ground in front of you. I believe in throwing the club aggressively into the ball with your right hand, but you'll only get power and accuracy if you release the club as if you were spreading those seeds.

Most casual golfers aren't inclined to follow the rules. It's a reflection of how society today views rules in general. If the people at Enron knew where the out-of-bounds stakes were, they wouldn't have wound up in a courtroom.

People today ask, "Is it legal or illegal?" We used to ask, "Is it right or wrong?"

A guy presented himself to me as being a "self-made man." I said, "You must be the first SOB who ever came out of the womb self-made." We all learn from other people. We need other people. I've had 30,000 teachers in my lifetime. We all have.

How many weddings were conducted at country clubs in the last year? Is 50,000 a good guess? Golf for some reason was chosen to stage all these things in society—real-estate developments, business meetings, civic functions, weddings, and so much else. Country clubs do a hell of a job. It irritates me when someone who doesn't know any better presents golf as the bad guy. The next time Martha Burk wants to throw a wedding, maybe she'll phone a handball court—and send invitations to the thousand women who played Augusta National the year before she attacked it.

I like helping tour players with their short games, but the full swing, forget it. I don't want them phoning me and calling me Coach. That is the last thing in the world I need. Or they need.

When a primitive hunter threw a spear at his prey, you better believe he followed through and finished with his weight on his left foot. Reverse pivots in the jungle could be fatal. That saber-toothed tiger would eat you. Any throwing motion requires a weight shift to the left. Stone Age man realized that. Millions of years later, poor golfers do not.

GREAT ALBERTO
THE STRONGEST MAN IN THE WOR
THE GREAT ALBERTO
THE STRONGEST MAN IN THE WORLD
75
150
150

Sean (the Beast) Fister

It's odd that some of the world's strongest, most violent athletes are, when removed from the stage, the gentlest creatures imaginable. That is the case with Sean Fister, a three-time National Long Drive champion who swings a club so ferociously that his drives can travel up to four hundred yards—through the air, not counting roll. Fister in person is not a beast at all. At his club outside Little Rock, Arkansas, he proves to be modest, self-effacing, considerate ("You sure the room isn't too cold? Want me to have them turn the heat up?"), and Old World polite. He loves his sport and grasps what "real" golfers (read: tour players) often do not—that the success of all professional sports ultimately depends on the athlete's willingness to promote it.

Fister is a physical curiosity. He has broken many bones, suffered many cuts and muscle tears, been beat up inside and out. Wonder at his pain threshold alone makes it hard to take your eyes off him, and a tour of his scars will make you wince. He grew up the hard way, in a large family in which the father was absent most of his life—the Fister kids often supped on bread and butter. He was left not hardened, but with a profound empathy for adults, a soft spot for children, and an ability to get an accurate read on people. Fister is one interview subject I left hoping I'd made a friend for life.

o o o

When I swing the club at 150 miles per hour and hit it absolutely pure, it feels like a whiff. The club is designed so that if I unload the shaft correctly and catch the ball dead in the middle of the sweet spot, the transfer of energy is so efficient that I feel nothing. In long driving, feedback is for losers.

My longest carry ever is 466 yards, at a course not far from Castle Pines in Colorado. A guy lasered it from the ball mark back to the tee. I prefer to measure that one not in distance but in hang time: It was in the air for twenty seconds. I'm very proud of that. Ronnie Lott, the football player, was one of the people standing there counting.

When I started out in long driving, persimmon drivers were still around. To this day the longest drive I've ever hit was with a Bert Dargie persimmon driver with a steel shaft. With a forty-mile-per-hour wind at my back and a firm fairway, I drove the ball three yards past the hole on a straightaway, 512-yard hole. Could have been a triple eagle, a hole in one on a par five. But I pulled it a bit.

With the new balls, persimmon won't hit it anywhere. I've tried.

I've hit people on courses before. Never with a crooked drive. It's always somebody on the green of a par 4. My playing partners get tired of waiting, and they goad me: "You can't reach them," and "It's okay, if you drive the green, I'll apologize for you." I've hit two people on the fly, one a guy I hit in the face and cut him around his eye and nose, another a lady I hit on the shoulder. They both went to the hospital. I've bounced balls into many people. I refuse to be goaded now and even give a speech: "You have to be patient with me because I've hit people before, and it's not pretty: It's fun to watch me hit it far, but it comes with a price."

When they say I hit the ball out of sight, for me it's literally true. I'm blind in my left eye because of macular degeneration. If it's overcast, I need some help telling me where my ball came down. Most of the time in competition I can tell by the sound and feel.

Freaky things happen when the clubhead is traveling more than 150 miles per hour. I mean crazy stuff, like the top of the driver flying off or the whole clubhead disintegrating. One time I shattered a clubhead, and a shard of metal flew up and hit me in the cheek. It cut me pretty deep. If it had hit me in my right eye, I'd be cooked.

I can't count how many driver heads I've caved in or the number of shafts I've broken. Thousands, I guess. Heck, I caved in or cracked forty-two faces at the World Long Drive Championship last year. At first I snapped the shafts about six inches up from the hosel. After the manufacturers started adding more boron down there, I started snapping them just below the grip. It's still a problem. If I had to pay for my shafts and clubheads, I'd be on welfare.

I've got too many drivers at my house. Roughly six hundred completed, and if you count the number of driver heads I have in boxes, it's over a thousand. The average person would be set for life. But the way I break them, I doubt what I have on hand would last a year.

In our sport, accuracy matters—a lot. The grid is only fifty-two yards wide, and when you're hitting the ball close to four hundred yards, your misses become exponentially worse. I've got to rein it in a little, or none of the six balls in my round will find the box.

I can play a little. I've had good days with tour players where they suggested I work on my game and take a crack at playing professionally. My best score is a 64, eight under par, here at Chenal, my club in Little Rock. My short game would probably surprise you; playing with Tommy Bolt in a charity tournament a while back, I chipped in three times. Tommy was dancing all over the place. "Sean is the greatest player in the world," he said to anybody who would listen. But I know how good tour players really are, and I'm smart enough to stick with what I know best.

On the wide-open course at Chenal my index is plus-1.3. On the tight one I'm five strokes worse, a 4. It's not that I'm crooked. It's that there's no place for one of my straight drives to land.

I make a good living. I do more than eighty appearances a year at up to $15,000 a crack, and I won $100,000 for my last win at the World Long Drive Championship. I make extra off endorsements. I'm not the richest guy in Arkansas, but we do have the full cable TV package, we have pizza delivered a couple of times a week, and none of our clothes have holes in them.

I've done a lot of clinics and exhibitions with John Daly, who's also from Arkansas, and he likes to point out that he has to go play his golf ball after he drives but I don't. What can I say? He's right. I like John. He can really move it, too, though he used to be a lot closer to me than he is now. My best against his best, I'd have to spot him at least thirty yards.

If you think the average Joe longs to hit the ball farther, you should see tour players. I imagine there are guys on the PGA Tour who would pay $300,000 for fifteen more yards of driving distance, because being that much closer to the green would put at least that much in their pocket. Most of them say the same thing: "If I hit it as far as you do, with no loss of accuracy, I'd shoot nothing." The quest for distance in golf is a drug, and tour players are the biggest addicts out there.

One day I did an outing at Bay Hill in Orlando. It so happened that my all-time hero in sports, Arnold Palmer, was there that day. I met him, and when he asked what I did for a living and I told him, he got a very devilish look on his face and asked if I'd like to play golf with him the next day. Of course I said yes. He then led me over to the starter and asked him to make room for one more—"and make sure Sean is on my team."

I barely slept that night. The next morning I was so excited I forgot to eat breakfast. That was bad news, and potentially dangerous because I'm hypoglycemic, so I get very weak and light-headed. When I got to Bay Hill I was hoping I could finagle some crackers from the restaurant before we teed off. I know it sounds silly, but it's not like you can ask your host, Arnold Palmer, to go get you a sandwich. But as I was walking toward the clubhouse, Mr. Palmer saw me and led me inside. He put his hand on my shoulder and looked at me with a knowing smile and asked—I swear he was reading my mind—"Sean, have you had anything to eat?" Was I ever relieved when he took me into the dining room. He then asked two members if they would sit with me while I ate, so I wouldn't have to eat alone. That lesson in consideration was the first of many things I learned from Mr. Palmer that day, which rates as one of the great days of my life.

The second lesson I learned from Mr. Palmer came after he pulled out my chair and seated me at the breakfast table. He leaned over and said in a kind, grandfatherly tone, "Sean, I know you're excited to be here. I'm going to do all I can to make it a great day for you." He paused for a moment and then laid the lesson on me: "Sean, after you eat but before you leave the table, you might want to consider zipping up the fly on your trousers."

I'm entirely self-taught. It's a good way to learn, but you do have moments of frustration and confusion. To fix that, I took seven years' worth of *Golf Digest*s and divided them into stacks on my kitchen table. I went through every one and wrote down every distance tip I came across. It took a while, and when I was finished I had 397 tips. I eliminated all of the duplications, then I went to work dealing with the tips that conflicted—stance, grip pressure, wrist cock, and so on. All of the contradictions I put to the test. Using each tip, I noted the balls I absolutely murdered. Tips that produced a ball in the "kill" column made the final list, which resides in a little black book I carry wherever I go. I call it the Bible.

There are a hundred little tricks to hit the ball farther. But only one is absolutely, positively guaranteed to work for every golfer. All you do is turn your shoulders farther, all the while keeping the butt end of the club as far away from your sternum as possible. It takes practice and physical effort, but if you work hard at that for two weeks, you'll for sure pick up twenty yards with the driver.

The best instruction tip I ever got came by accident. On ESPN Classic one night they were replaying one of Nolan Ryan's no-hitters. He was throwing serious heat, almost nothing but fastballs. I noticed that before every pitch, he would wiggle, shake, and rotate his right hand and wrist. It struck me he was trying to put oil in them, to make them as relaxed as possible so he could throw the ball faster. That turned a light on for me. I went out the next morning and, keeping my shoulders, arms, and hands as relaxed as I could, thought only of swinging the club fast through impact. Almost without trying, I hit some of the longest drives of my life. Straight, too. When I'm fluid and relaxed, I'm very dangerous.

Before I earned the nickname the Beast for the distance I could hit a softball, I was known as the Pipe Wrench. For a time I laid pipe for a utility company, and on one of my first days a water line broke. While a couple of guys ran off to get a pipe wrench, I unscrewed the pipe with my hands. When they came back and saw what I had done, they stood there with their mouths open. I was the Pipe Wrench from that day forward.

The other thing I could do was work a jackhammer like nobody else. A jackhammer weighs seventy-five pounds, and after it penetrates a layer of asphalt, the bit gets wedged in tight. It takes the average construction worker a couple of good pulls to yank it out and start on a new spot. Well, I fell in love with the jackhammer. I once worked a mile-long stretch of asphalt in a day, which made me a legend of sorts. What it did for my forearms you can see if you tune in.

I'm six-five and weigh 245. When I started out in the early '90s I was one of the bigger guys. At the finals this year I looked up at more than half of them. John Colborne is six-nine. Kurt Moore is six-seven. Viktor Johansson is six-seven and weighs 275, and his arms are as big around as my head. He's a lumberjack type more than a pure athlete. The days of someone other than a physical superman winning are over. I seriously doubt whether anyone under six-two will ever win again.

Long drivers as a group are big people, but because we dress like golfers, I guess that makes us suspect. A bunch of us were in a bar in Phoenix drinking beer a few years back when some big construction guys walked in and sat near us. After they'd had some beers, one of them came over to the table and said, "Any one of you guys like to arm wrestle? I got twenty dollars that says I can take any one of you." None of our guys came forward, which embarrassed me.

"Hell, I'll go you for twenty dollars," I said. So they cleared an area and squared us off across one of the tables.

When one of his guys said, "Go!" my opponent moved my arm a little and gave me a pathetic look. At that point I slammed his arm down hard—*pow!* My opponent said it was a fluke and demanded a rematch, so we did it again, and I beat him again, this time faking a yawn while I put him down.

What nobody knew was, I'd helped put myself through college tearing up guys by arm wrestling in bars. Be careful who you challenge in life. Size matters, but it doesn't tell you everything.

The most intimidating person I've ever met was Bo Jackson. I was playing in George Brett's charity tournament when Bo's group came through. The airline had lost his luggage, and he wasn't in an especially great mood. I said something to him, and when he looked up at me I saw the face of a shark, like there was no human he couldn't tear apart if he put his mind to it. If you were in a war, you'd want Bo Jackson at your side.

Bill Clinton is from Arkansas, and we've played together several times. He's the most intent listener I've ever encountered; talking to him is almost intimidating because you have his undivided attention, and you can tell he's weighing every word you say. He also has a phenomenal memory. Several years passed between visits, and when I saw him again, he asked how my wife was—he remembered her name—how my two children were doing, and how was my back feeling? He's a remarkable man by any measure. When I saw him a few months ago, he looked ten years older than I expected.

A lot of great athletes believe that proper mental preparation sets the stage for great physical performance. I've found it to work the other way around. By training very hard physically, I find it much easier to reach the state of mind necessary to perform my very best.

I practice hitting drivers three hundred days a year. Most every morning I'm on the ninth tee at Chenal, hitting drivers from seven to nine-fifteen, when the first group comes through. I then go straight to the range and hit for another hour or two, then take a break. I then hit all afternoon. Nothing but drivers; as many as a thousand balls a day. It's my job, man, and I work at it. On my days off I'm at the gym. Very rarely do I have a day where I don't beat balls.

The purpose of hitting that many drivers is to reach what I call "hitting shape." It's the razor-edge level of physical conditioning that's unique to my sport. It's a combination of flexibility, strength, speed, and stamina that can be obtained only through hitting many, many balls. No regimen at the gym can replace it. Have you ever hit so many balls that your muscles become fatigued and you start hitting the ball shorter instead of longer? The purpose of being in hitting shape is to guarantee that my thousandth ball in a day goes as far as my first.

It's through repetitions that you find answers. A good example of that was at the 1997 Long Drive Championship. I was in great hitting shape, but my technique was poor. On the day of the finals I started hitting on the range at ten a.m., and at ten-thirty Mike Gorton showed up. He hit for forty-five minutes, then said, "I'm going for some lunch and a nap. You coming back out later?" I told him I would, at around four.

When Mike came back at four, I was there waiting for him, hitting drivers.

"When did you come back out?" he asked.

"I never left," I said.

Mike said, "Beast, what the hell are you doing? You'll have nothing left for tonight!"

I told Mike, "I'd rather be tired and hitting it good than be rested and hitting it bad. And I'm real close."

In the semis that night, I caved in the face of a great driver head. I had only one good head left, and it was on a shaft I didn't like, so I had to change it over. The finals were twelve minutes away. I got the head off, drilled out the hosel, applied the glue to the shaft and stuck it in the hosel. It was cold outside, the epoxy wouldn't dry and the head wouldn't set. I was in a panic; showtime was only a couple of minutes away. I dove into my van, turned the heat on full blast and held the driver against the vents. After a few seconds, the head locked and I ran out to my spot just in time to hit. My first ball went 406, but it barely rolled into a bunker in the grid. Jason Zuback blasted a big one, and it rolled out to 412. He nipped me, but the tension and pressure was great.

What muscles do you want to develop to get more distance? The shoulder girdle is huge, on the left shoulder especially. On the left arm it's the triceps, the right arm the inner triceps and the biceps. The most important muscle of all is the muscle that meets your biceps on top of your forearm, the one that bulges near that sharp bone on top near your elbow. See mine? It's similar to Mark McGwire's. That's the muscle that will win or lose for you.

My driver heads have anywhere from three to six degrees of loft, which doesn't sound like much. But I try to hit the ball slightly on the upswing, and the shaft kicks the head forward before impact, and that adds even more loft. It takes serious swing speed to take advantage of those factors. The average player would be lucky to hit anything more than a line drive with one of my clubs.

My driver is forty-eight inches long. I've hit a sixty-inch driver, and one ball out of fifty I hit went thirty to forty yards farther than my best pop with my regular driver, but I couldn't control it. If I were standing in the center of a giant bull's-eye and could blast the ball across concentric circles, I'd go with a longer shaft. But like I say, long driving is somewhat like real golf. Accuracy does matter.

Truth be told, I think all long drive competitions should be limited to a forty-five-inch driver. In performing exhibitions, I've found that average golfers can relate better to normal-size clubs. They appreciate my ability more, even though the ball flies shorter than with my forty-eight-inch model.

If you miss the sweet spot by a quarter of an inch, you'll lose maybe 5 percent of your distance. To me that's fatal, because 5 percent of four hundred is twenty, and I can't afford to give twenty yards to the monsters I go up against. Same with keeping the clubface square. If my clubface is open or closed two degrees, I'm a dead man.

Tommy Bolt and I hit it off so well he invited me up to his ranch to hunt deer. I was so excited the night before I couldn't sleep. Tommy came by my cabin to pick me up at four-thirty a.m., and boy, was I excited about going deer hunting with Mr. Bolt. He drove me in his golf cart over to a tree stand—we're hunting right on his property, remember—and he says, "Good luck. I'll pick you up in five hours." I said, "Great, Mr. Bolt. Where's your tree stand?" He said, "Hell, son, I ain't hunting no deer. I'm going back to bed!" And with that he drove off.

My dad left us when I was seven. There were seven of us kids under age thirteen, and he didn't help out with child support. You can imagine how tough that situation was on my mother. Somehow she got it done. She was small, but she ruled the house with an iron fist. We used to say that it was her arm on the box of Arm & Hammer baking soda. But there was only so much she could do. My two older brothers went to prison—drug-related things. The rest of us turned out all right, and four of us went to college on athletic scholarships, but when I think of my brothers, who are talented, good-looking, athletic guys, it makes me feel bad for her. She deserved for all of us to become standout people in life.

There was no way my mother could afford to put me through college. Thankfully I learned how to pole vault, and it won me a scholarship to the University of Florida. I also competed in the decathlon, but everything revolved around the pole vault, and it very nearly killed me. Before arriving in Florida, I had a late growth spurt and shot up three inches and gained a lot of weight. My size was a big problem because I started breaking a lot of poles.

When you break poles, you get hurt. My back, my right foot, my left foot, cartilage in both knees. I cracked my skull on the edge of the pit on a bad vault, and another time I almost lost my left thumb. But I had to do it. It was either jump or give up my scholarship and go back home to a life of

who knows what. Desperation will make a person do things he wouldn't ordinarily do.

All I've done playing golf is tear both rotator cuffs. As a result of that and my pole-vaulting adventures, I've become an expert on anti-inflammatory drugs. I gulp more naproxen than I should, because it can wreak havoc with your liver. But I won't be a long-driving champion forever, and taking over-the-counter medication sure beats taking twenty-four cortisone shots a year, which I did one year when I was banged up. When I'm finished competing, I hope the naproxen is going in the garbage can.

The characters who show up to take a bite at the apple in our competitions seem to be getting stranger. The weirdest show up at the local level. A guy showed up a while back who weighed 280 and wore a tank top and spandex shorts. I don't wish anybody ill, but when he got up to hit I said a silent prayer: *Please, Lord, don't let this guy advance to the finals. Our sport deserves better than this.* But the more I thought about it, the more I thought how this guy might be just what we need. We're a grass-roots sport. It's entertainment. We can use a little color.

I have a fantasy. I'd like to get a bunch of long-drive buddies together, get geared up, head out to the course, and play a golf-ball version of paint ball. A test of skill, accuracy, and power. I can hit a ball through a three-quarter-inch sheet of plywood, so we'd have to gear up good. But it'd be a blast.

Even if I catch a ball dead on the button, it's possible someone out there can outdrive me. But it hasn't happened yet.

Curtis Strange

In his best years, during the mid- to late 1980s, writers became accustomed to approaching Curtis gingerly. He always seemed wound to 110 compression, his intensity part of what earned him back-to-back U.S. Open titles in 1988 and 1989. He did not suffer fools gladly. But Curtis nowadays is easygoing and downright fun to be around, with a self-effacing sense of humor and teasing nature. I met with him in 2005 during a now-defunct event called the UBS Warburg Cup, in which a team of U.S. senior players took on a team from the rest of the world. We got carried away, and Curtis showed up late for the team photo. When he arrived, amid catcalls and loud scoldings from his teammates, he flushed with embarrassment. Deciding to add an egg-beater to troubled waters, I stood facing the team and said, "Sorry I got him here late, guys, but Curtis told me this wasn't very important." The murderous look he gave me was priceless.

○ ○ ○

The day I turned pro, I was $10,000 in debt. My father had passed away when I was fourteen, and by the time I left college, money was an issue. I'd borrowed the money to play my last year of amateur golf, and when I turned pro I was living hand to mouth, trying like hell to pay off that loan. There was a lot of pressure, but a lot of guys from that era were used to that and rolled with it. I'd had a job in high school, and I figured if golf didn't work out, I'd just get another job, hopefully in the golf business. I'm not saying my values are any better than pro athletes you see today, but for better or worse most of them have never had a real job.

I was a good shoe salesman. That was some job, a world within a world. To this day, I can tell someone's shoe size by taking one glance at their feet. You wear an eight and a half, I can tell. Would you like some polish or socks to go with those, sir?

When a child loses a parent, he tends to carry one memory that stands out above all others. For me there was a day when I was totally lost and frustrated about my swing. Dad was the head pro, and I was hesitant to bother him while he was working. But one afternoon, after three miserable days trying to fix whatever problem I had, I walked into his office and asked him to help me. As I began explaining my problem, I started crying. He could be firm, but this time he put his arm around me and walked me out to the range. He spent the rest of the afternoon working with me. We didn't have many moments where it was just him and me, and this day was something very special. It makes me happy to look back on that moment, but it hurts some, too, because it makes me miss him all over again.

Some pros are harder to play with than others, and the worst was Seve Ballesteros. To say he was difficult is an understatement. To a man, every player who went up against him in the Ryder Cup had a run-in with him. His gamesmanship was irritating, and he never let up. He'd do outrageous, childish things like coughing as you got set to swing, and if you objected he'd act wounded and escalate the situation. When he put himself into the role of victim, that's when he'd play his best. Just knowing he'd use a nasty incident to play well made me so mad that I'd play worse. There was only one Seve, and a little of him went a long way. But I'll tell you this, he could back it up. If you were 0–5 against a guy, that stuff would hack you off, too.

Nick Faldo stared a lot of guys down. He never choked. He had a way of folding his arms and looking at you as though he knew you were going to make a mistake. And guys would screw up against him. But in our playoff at Brookline [1988 U.S. Open], I was in a good frame of mind to handle Nick. We didn't say three words all day, which was fine with me. My feeling was, "I'll wait for you to hiccup." And he did hiccup—he bogeyed number eleven, which gave me a two-shot lead—and I beat him. Faldo got the better of me a couple of times, at the Ryder Cup especially, but I got him at the big one when he was in his prime. I'm proud of that.

Going for my third consecutive U.S. Open, I was two shots back going into the last round. I didn't play very well and didn't win. I was in the car with [wife] Sarah and my brother, Allan, when the realization hit me that it was over—that two-year run of being the Open champion. I'd had a ball being on top of the world, but the feeling when it ended was an odd mix of emptiness and total relief.

Allan and I roomed together at the British Open at Birkdale in 1991. Thursday morning came around and we woke up at about the same time. "You get in the shower first," I said. "I think I'll just lie here." Normally I was up stomping around, raring to get to the course.

That was the first evidence of what I now suspect might have been depression. It pretty much spelled the end of my career as a productive player. I got headaches, felt lethargic and fatigued. The last thing I wanted to do was play golf. It may have been a virus of some kind, but after reading about the experiences of Terry Bradshaw [former NFL quarterback], I think it was depression, the outcome of having so many highs and lows over the years. Gradually I worked my way out of it, but it was devastating.

People ask me what it's like to have an identical twin. Hell, it's all Allan and I ever knew, so how do I answer that? I do know I had a playmate, competitor, and best friend at my side every day of my life. Now I'm jealous because he plays more golf than I do.

For twenty years I talked with Allan every Sunday night. He's the only man I know who'll give me an honest answer.

Everybody has an opinion on what's wrong with Tiger's swing, but what fascinates me is his stubbornness, his reluctance to

take a step back and say, "Maybe this plan isn't working." Tiger's a smart person, very sharp. But his stubbornness, which in one form or another is a trait of every great champion, cuts both ways. It helps, and it can hurt.

My biggest regret is that I didn't play in the British Open when I was at my best. Why did I stay home? Because people told

me I had to go. Like I said, stubbornness helps, and it can hurt.

Proudest moment of my career: winning the NCAA Championship at Wake Forest. Seriously. We were a great team. *Golf World* named us the best college team of all time, and that's saying a lot. Jay Haas was there; Bob Byman, who won at Bay Hill after he turned pro, was there; a lot of great amateur golfers. We were young, we were cocky, and the world was uncomplicated. Talk to a lot of pros, and they'll tell you the best time of their lives was playing college golf.

I wasn't a particularly good student. Only good enough to stay eligible. I'm not real proud of that.

Jay Haas—mild-mannered and unassuming, "nicest guy on tour" and all that, right? Wrong. He's the best practical joker of all time, pure evil when it comes to knowing my weak spots and pushing my buttons. At Wake he was just relentless. Once, after I'd putted poorly in a college tournament, he conned me into believing the Bulls Eye putter I loved was a bad putter for me. So I stuck it out the window of the van and ground it down to nothing on the pavement while we were going seventy miles per hour. Then he said he was just kidding, and why did I go and ruin my best putter? These things made me want to kill him, but I couldn't retaliate because I wasn't as sly or witty as he was. I'd just stew. Jay loved it and still does—when he's around, I keep one eye open for fear of what he might say or do next. He's the only person alive who has my number.

Where do I stand on the technology debate? Modern equipment has gotten out of control. I have to carry my cell phone, extra battery, earpiece, and battery charger wherever I go. I need my laptop, charger, and wires. The manufacturers promised these things would make life easier; instead they've added three hours to my day. Where does it end?

I like forged-blade irons better than cavity-back clubs, partly because they feel so soft

when I hit a shot right on the button. But I also like them because a poorly struck shot makes your hands ring. Bad shots should cause you all sorts of pain.

At the course where I grew up, I played with gamblers all the time, with my father's blessing. The money wasn't huge, but five dollars was enough to get my attention. I've always felt you should have something riding every time you play. Betting is crucial to a young player's development.

Our guys just aren't as excited about the Ryder Cup as they used to be, certainly not as excited as the Europeans, who always are motivated by beating the big, bad USA. For an American who plays in one of these things every year—there's the Presidents Cup, too—it's only a matter of time before you blow a big match and get fried by the media. For guys like Tiger and Mickelson it's not just about playing for their country, it's about getting scrutinized and hammered if they don't play well. If I had to make a prediction, I'd say the Europeans will win next time, too. Pride will take over eventually. The Americans will get sick of getting beat. But that's still a ways off.

Here's the deal on my leaving ABC: They wanted a two-year commitment from me beginning this year, which also is my rookie year on the Champions Tour. I said, "Okay, but if I'm going to cut back on the opportunity to make money playing, I need an extra commitment from you." I wanted to be part of their next contract with the PGA Tour as well. That was too much for them, and like I've said, I was disappointed. Doing TV is easier than playing golf. I've slept better at night the last several years. The knots in my stomach are gone. You still have to get the job done on Sunday, but it's easier doing that from the booth than on the golf course.

I got fined by the tour for using bad language a few times. What's interesting is, I hear language on TV sitcoms today that's as bad as the things I got fined for.

Nothing tastes better than the first beer after a long day of shopping with Sarah. Or maybe the second beer, because I drink the first one so fast it doesn't touch the sides of my throat.

Greg Norman

Getting ninety minutes alone with Greg Norman takes some doing. In this case I flew to San Juan, Puerto Rico, and caught a connecting flight to the distant Caribbean island of Anguilla, where Norman was designing a golf course. After walking the entire shell of the golf course—and then walking it backward—we retired to a small villa for our conversation. Norman was loose, and the talk was excellent. He discussed his near misses in a helicopter and scuba diving, a fistfight he'd once narrowly avoided, some lore on koala bears and kangaroos, and his unusual sixth sense for knowing where he is in space. Sixty minutes into our conversation, someone knocked on the door and said there was something on the course that needed a second look: "Sorry, mate, gotta go." And gone he was. Initially I was chafed that the interview was cut short, but after I transcribed the tape, I found he'd given me plenty. When you had Norman's attention, his conversation was like his golf game—powerful, efficient, and creative.

○ ○ ○

As a young man, I used to have a dream where I was stuck in the corner of a room, a big boulder was rolling toward me, and there was nowhere to go. I'd wake up and think, *Maybe that boulder represents the world, and it's getting bigger, and there are all kinds of opportunity coming my way.* Then I'd think, *Maybe that boulder is the world, and it's going to smash me to death.* I stopped having the dream by working so hard during the day that I couldn't dream at night—or at least couldn't remember the dream when I woke up.

I used to be in awe of Seve Ballesteros and the way he'd deliberately hook or slice the ball sixty yards. He was the best shotmaker I ever saw. We'll never see the likes of him again, because the equipment won't allow it. It's very hard to make the modern ball curve. You've heard this before, usually from a seventy-year-old guy who you think is just pining for the good old days. But I'm telling you, equipment has made the game less spectacular to watch.

Most amateurs would die to be able to spin the ball backward, but for a pro there's no problem as frustrating as spinning the ball too much. During the mid-'80s I played the Tour Edition ball, which spun like no ball before or since. The third hole at Augusta National was a nightmare for me. There just was no place to land the ball and keep it on the green. Once, not knowing what else to do, I landed my ball on the right side of the green and spun it sideways ninety feet to the left, to where the pin was. The Tour Edition helped me win the 1986 British Open at Turnberry, because the greens were like rocks, and it was the only ball that would hold. But it killed me in majors in America, including more than one Masters, because the damn thing spun so much.

I'm in a helicopter with my wife just west of Sydney. It's a hot day, we've got a full passenger load, and we're full of fuel. We came in too hot speedwise for a tight landing zone near some apple trees. Suddenly alarms went off as the pilot tried to correct his mistake. The tail rotor hit the ground, and he tried to pull back, which lurched us forward into the apple orchard. At the last minute, he reduced power and dropped us on the ground. It felt like when I landed on an aircraft carrier. Laura was stunned; I was furious. I really lit into that pilot, who didn't seem to comprehend how close we'd come to buying the farm.

If we're three-dimensional figures and throw a two-dimensional shadow, why aren't we the shadow of the fourth dimension? What I'm saying is, had I died in that helicopter crash, there's another life after this one.

Steve Elkington and I had just finished dinner with our hosts at a restaurant in Portland a while back. We're walking to our cars, and a group of guys recognize us and start giving us a hard time. I've been in that situation before, and the best thing to do is walk away. Steve, though, held his ground. Unlike a lot of guys in that situation, he was ready to get it on. We finally got everybody in the car, and we peeled out of there.

Now the guys follow us down the freeway and start throwing beer bottles at the car. We finally ditched them. It was an exciting night for our hosts. That's all they talked about the rest of our stay. I had a hard time making them believe that I get this stuff from time to time. I don't know what it is. Maybe people don't like the way I look.

Don't piss off a kangaroo. He'll stand on his tail and kick hell out of you with his big feet, which have huge toenails. Don't fool with a koala bear, either. You look at one and want to put him next to your pillow, but climb a tree and mess with him and you've got a problem. Sharks you already know about.

You don't know pain until you've had the bends. Not long ago I was scuba diving eighty-eight feet under the surface, chasing a fish, and caught my regulator on an overhanging rock. It was punctured, and I didn't know it. Suddenly I'm in big trouble. I either had to find my buddy or ascend fast, or I'd suffocate. I chose the ascent, but knowing that air in my lungs would expand as I went up. I made it out and into the boat just in time. Lying there, it felt like someone put my joints in a vice. It was a mild case of the bends, but even then it was almost more than I could bear.

That huge power outage in the Northeast last year hit during the PGA at Oak Hill. I had just come off the golf course. The house I was staying in had no power for hours. It was so peaceful. We found some candles and improvised dinner. We left the house on a quest for ice to keep our beer cold; we laughed and felt satisfied when we found some. The best part was, my cell phone didn't work. It was like camping out. I loved it.

You may remember when Bruce Edwards left Tom Watson for a time and came to work for me. We became very close friends, which happens more rarely than you might think. Caddie-player relationships tend to run their course, however, and Bruce and I knew exactly when that point had come. It was a Friday at Milwaukee. I'd had a bad run of playing and was mad at myself and getting short-tempered with Bruce. Standing in the car-park area, we looked at each other and knew what the other guy was thinking. Bruce said, "Maybe we should go our separate ways." I told him I agreed, and we both shed some tears. Bruce went back to Tom, and I think there was a happy destiny in that, because with all Bruce is going through, there is no better man to be there for him than Tom.

My exposure to some of the best financial minds in the world taught me one thing: Never put your money at risk. When you sign your name on the bottom line, make sure you aren't the guarantor of anything. Invest in things where, in a worst-case scenario, you don't get the return you hoped for, but still get a return.

Tiger is almost halfway to Jack's record in the majors. I've got a feeling the second half will be much harder than the first. See, great players have always appeared every ten years. Arnold Palmer is ten years older than Jack, who's ten years older than Watson. Bobby Jones was ten years older than Nelson, Hogan, and Snead, who were the same age. Somewhere there's a kid—maybe several of them—exactly ten years younger than Tiger, who's twenty-eight. They're working hard on their games and dreaming of nothing else but being the best. In five years they're going to make it very, very hard for Tiger. Will he break the record? Time will tell.

Some players have good hand/eye coordination. Others have feel. My strength was a sense of where I am in space and a feel for the things around me. Depth perception, sensing where the wind is coming from and how hard it's blowing, how firm a green is just by looking at it, that sort of thing. You can spin me around in a dark room, and when you stop I can tell you which way north is. When I hunt or fish in the wild or go scuba diving, I have no apprehension about my surroundings. When you play with someone who seems to be a "natural," they often have this sense.

I wouldn't mind seeing the Presidents Cup and Ryder Cup joined into a truly international three-way competition. But the PGA Tour, which controls the Presidents Cup, would have to concede some control, and the people there don't want to give up control of anything. I found that out when I tried to start a form of the World Golf Championships. I was knocked down by the PGA Tour and told it would be bad for golf, only to watch the people there create the very thing I had in mind. With the PGA Tour, it's all about control.

Bob Tway holing it from the bunker, I could live with. It was a shot that a good pro holes fairly often. Robert Gamez and David Frost holing out to beat me, they hurt, but I got over them. The one that killed me inside was Larry Mize's chip at the Masters. That was destiny saying, *You aren't going to win this tournament.*

In high school the teacher would give us the cane. If you got out of line, out would come the bamboo cane, five feet long. They made you hold out your hands, and *whack*! The number of whacks depended on the severity of the offense. Man, did that smart. I don't look back on it as being particularly barbaric. It was fair, effective discipline.

When I turn fifty, I might play in the senior majors, but that's it. One reason I developed outside business interests was so I wouldn't be dependent on playing to make a living. And it might be a moot point—the Champions Tour might not even exist by the time I turn fifty.

I was for Casey Martin, big time. The PGA Tour blew it, Jack Nicklaus and Arnold Palmer blew it. I thought it was disgraceful. They forgot to ask themselves one question: What if he were my own son?

Some golfers are consistently lucky. They hit their ball in the trees, and as you help them look for it, you get the feeling you'll not only find the ball, but they'll have a good lie and an opening. Sure enough, they do. The luckiest golfer I've known is Freddie Couples. Ask Fred; he'll admit he's lucky. My luck is average, with a couple of the bad breaks happening at crucial times.

I can still win a major. I'll try like heck to get to the Masters this year, and if that doesn't work out, I'll try to prequalify for the U.S. Open, because Shinnecock Hills is my favorite golf course. My best chance will always be at the British Open.

The best ball flight in golf is a power fade. A draw-type swing with the face a shade open at impact. My whole career I aimed at the left edge of the rough and swung as hard as I could. I never worried about the ball going left. I've had my problems, but driving the ball long and straight has never been one of them.

I don't like to guarantee anything—that it won't rain tomorrow, that the new washing machine won't break down the next time I use it, or that I'll hole a six-inch putt. The only guarantee I make is that I'll follow through on a commitment I've made. Even that's dangerous, because I might not wake up tomorrow.

Moe Norman

I'd heard that Moe Norman was far more comfortable with children than he was with adults, and the rumor was validated when I walked into the coffee shop of Carlisle Golf Club in Toronto. There was Moe at a table playing a game with a five-year-old girl. The game was hard to figure out; it seemed to involve switching four golf balls from hand to hand. But Moe understood it and the girl did, and when I interrupted to introduce myself, Moe looked up at me with dread as though I were holding a bone saw. When we sat down, with a good friend of Moe's there for support and prompting, my gentle probings softened his distrust. Gradually Moe spouted pure gold. Of all my visits, the one with Moe was the most special. Not all of what he said came across well in print; his straight quotes made little sense, and when I annotated his words too much I lost his voice. But the better part of Moe came through, and just in time, too. The purest ball striker of all time died less than a month later.

○ ○ ○

I'm good with numbers. Number of courses played: 434. Number of courses I can remember the exact hole yardages: 375. Age when I saw my first doctor: 68. Number of two-stroke penalties in one eleven-year period: only one—I hit a drive that went out of bounds by two feet. Most balls hit in one day: 2,207. Total balls hit in my lifetime: About five million, not counting chips and putts.

I don't go to church, but I certainly pray a lot. Always have. One of my sisters was a nun, and when I was young my parents dragged me to church by the seat of my pants. God is real—He has to be, because no man could develop the talent I have on his own. I am the world's best ball striker and teacher because it was His will. Why did He choose me to be the best who ever lived? I don't have the faintest idea. That's why there's a hereafter—so one day I can find out.

One day I met Dave Pelz, the short-game teacher. We were debating, and I told him I could drive the ball straighter than he could putt one. He looked at me funny, and I told him I was serious. "Let's put a post out in the fairway 250 yards away. You choose a hole to putt at from eighty feet away. We'll take turns, and I bet I'll hit the post before you hole a putt." Dave turned down the bet. Dave is going around telling this story, so you know it's true.

I hated putting, and so did George Knudson, another really good ball striker on tour. We played against each other in many betting games where putting didn't count. If you missed a fairway, you owed the other guy twenty dollars. If you missed a green, you owed twenty dollars. If you hit the flagstick, you won a hundred dollars. When we got to the green we just picked up our balls and went to the next hole. George was very good, but I got the best of him. My best day, I hit the flagstick six times.

One year I was leading the Saskatchewan Open by three strokes. I was putting for birdie on the last hole, but just to see if I could handle the pressure, I deliberately putted my ball into the bunker. I looked at the side of the green and saw two guys with the blood drained from their faces. After I got up and down for a bogey to win by two strokes, I walked over and asked them what was the matter. "We had a huge bet on you to win," one of them said. "Sorry," I said. "I needed the variety."

Working on your swing is the greatest joy in golf. Tiger Woods must be having a wonderful time searching for that one little thing he's doing wrong. I wonder when he'll notice it—the way his right heel lifts straight off the ground now instead of coming up and toward his left. His weight shift is terrible right now, that's all. Don't tell him. It'll ruin his fun.

I'm seventy-five and I've never owned a telephone. Never needed one. You reached me, and here you are, right?

My given name is Murray. When I started out as a caddie, a guy started calling me Moe. Actually, he called me "Moe the Schmoe, the Pinochle Pro." It made no sense, but it stuck.

I'm good at tapping the ball on the face of my driver. One day a guy accused me of showing off, and then he wanted to make a bet. He said he'd give me a dollar for every bounce over a hundred. I got well over a hundred, and the guy's face turned white as a sheet. I was laughing so hard that I stopped at 192. I didn't have the heart to take more than that off him.

I hit so many balls I tend to build up a huge callus on the meaty part of my left hand. It gets so thick that from time to time I take a pair of scissors and cut it off. The edge of the callus gets very sharp—if I dragged it across your face I'd draw blood.

Speaking of calluses, the first time I saw Ben Hogan was at the Carling World Open at Oakland Hills. He was on the range, and all the players gathered to watch him. Hogan didn't notice because he was really concentrating, but when he finished he looked up and saw all the guys watching him. As he walked away, he said, "I can see why you guys are no good—you've all got calluses on your asses."

I shot 59 three times. The best of them I shot playing with the future U.S. Amateur champion Gary Cowan at Rockway Golf Course [in Ontario] in 1957. It could have been lower if I hadn't three-putted the tenth hole. In fact, I didn't putt all that well that day. I hit the ball close a lot, is all.

I just learned to putt a short time ago, and now I putt so well it would make you cry. It's the best part of my game, and that's saying a lot.

My childhood was very difficult. We were poor. Me and my brothers used bobby pins to hold our pants up, and we taped our shoes to hold them together. Our father was very strict. When I got a set of clubs together, he wouldn't let me bring them in the house. I knew if he got his hands on them he'd throw them out, so I kept them under the back porch, through a little hole where he couldn't get at them because he was fat. He was pleased when I started getting my name in the newspaper, but he never saw me hit a golf ball, even in our hometown when I became well known.

Even in my late teens and early twenties, when I got good enough to play in tournaments, I slept in bunkers and hitchhiked to get from one place to the next. Some of the golfers laughed like hell at me and teased me constantly—"Where you sleeping tonight, Moe?" Nobody came to my rescue until I was twenty-six. I really resented that.

In the 1950s there was no money to be made playing professionally in Canada. I stayed an amateur, working as a pinsetter in a bowling alley all winter so I could play golf all summer. This was before they had machines that set the pins. That was hard work, but, boy, was I good at it. I was able to work four lanes at once because they played with five pins, not ten. I hopped from one lane to the next like a bumblebee. No one was faster or better than me.

When money was dear, I'd play with the same ball until it wore out. A balata-covered wound ball had exactly five rounds in it before it got knocked out of round or got too soft. Then it was time to search the bushes for lost balls and root out a new one.

In the 1980s and early '90s I went through another hard time. The Canadian tour lost its sponsor, and for a while I had to sleep in my car. Then I went to the PGA Merchandise Show in Orlando. I was at the Titleist booth when Mr. [Wally] Uihlein, the CEO, walked up to me. "I see you're still wearing our visor and wear our FootJoy shoes," he said. "You've played our ball for forty years. Has anyone done anything for you?" I told him nobody had done anything, and that I'd never asked. Mr. Uihlein said, "Give me your hand." He gave me a handshake and said, "You're going to get $5,000 a month from us for the rest of your life." That was a big help. Between that and the start of the Natural Golf teaching program, I opened my first bank account.

I never got married. In fact, I went on only three dates. If I'd gotten married, it wouldn't have been fair to a wife because of my life as a golfer. I'd wind up divorced, and then she'd get everything. I think that's how it works, judging by what's happened to some friends of mine. I'm very happy being alone.

What would I do if I won the lottery and twenty million dollars? Give it away, probably to one of my relatives, even though they never cared enough about me to come and watch me play golf.

I don't like these superlong par 3s where average golfers need a wood to reach them. They're terrible—you hit fifteen or more wood shots on the other holes already; that's enough. On the other hand, I don't like par 4s where guys hit irons off the tee. What are these architects thinking about? They're designing courses upside down. They think they're smart, but they're just the opposite.

Backing the ball up on the green may look impressive, but it's no way to play golf, because you can't control it. Every shot you hit should bounce forward after it lands. If the flagstick is just over a bunker, you get it close by hitting the ball higher, not by backing it up. With these sixty-degree wedges, hitting it high is easy.

I don't understand why anyone would go to the gym to get in shape to play golf. If you hit six hundred balls a day, walk a lot and watch your diet, you'll get in shape. I don't think Sam Snead ever went to the gym, and nobody today is in better shape than he was. Hitting balls is the best workout there is.

I don't believe in taking much of a divot, especially with the longer irons. You want to barely comb the grass through impact, as though you were hitting a ball off the top of somebody's crew cut. It's the only way to catch the ball on the second groove up from the bottom of the clubface. That's where you want to make contact—on the second groove.

I never saw a doctor until I was sixty-eight. It's because I never felt sick. Never had a headache, earache, or toothache, and never had a cold. Then one day I had a heart attack. Now I see the doctor every day. All he did was make me give up all the foods I like, meaning liver and onions, hamburgers, hot dogs, chocolate, and barbecue potato chips, all that stuff. He made me switch from regular Coke—I drank fifteen cans a day on average—to caffeine-free Diet Coke. I've lost forty-five pounds, gone from a forty-two-inch waist to thirty-seven. But I sure miss that food.

I was in the clubhouse at Rockway Golf Course, and I overheard a kid telling another kid that he'd left his wedge at another course and that no one had turned it in. I went to my car and got him one, and he was so happy he jumped all over me. I do this often, especially with kids you can tell are a bit poor and don't get these things from their parents. Very often they start crying, they're so happy.

Crouching down to read a putt is a waste of time. So is plumb-bobbing. You can see all you need standing behind the ball and can feel the slope through your feet when you stand over the ball.

Going through the ball, I feel my right hand is a claw. No hinging of my right wrist at all. I just gather the ball up. No supination or pronation. On the follow-through I shake hands with the flagstick.

Don't hold the club lightly. That's a mistake, because you'll get too wristy. Hold it firmly. You won't hit the ball quite as far, but you'll hit it straighter, which is what this game is about.

If I had a bunch of juniors, I'd teach them to play from the green backward. Short shots first, with emphasis on how to meet the ball solidly. I'd make them touch the green, then walk backward to the tee and touch the tee, and explain why holes are designed the way they are. Then I'd teach them why everything works—why a putter has so little loft, why the sand wedge is thicker on the bottom than a pitching wedge, and why woods are larger than irons. Those things mean something.

Then I'd help them feel the game. Whisper when they hit a ball solid, "Did you feel that? That's what you want." After a time—there's no hurry—I'd finally help them learn the game. That's the technical part. That comes last.

I hit so many balls I wore out three sets of irons. I'd wear the grooves down to nothing and then go even farther, so there was a concave area the size of a dime on the sweet spot. Eventually the ball would start to fly a little crooked from catching the sides of that pockmark, and the clubs became illegal because the faces weren't flat.

George Knudson loved to see 2s on his scorecard because they don't add up very fast. It wasn't unusual for George to score eight 2s during the course of a tournament. It wasn't a bad strategy. He was a good fairway-wood player, so he birdied a lot of par 5s, and that combined with his performance on the par 3s made him very competitive.

The heavier the clubs the better. The swingweight on all my clubs is E-3, and my driver weighs 16 ounces. To get them that heavy, I put lead tape under the grips and on the clubhead. I don't like light clubs. They feel like matchsticks to me and tend to wave all over the place when you swing them. Speed is important, but so is mass.

Try smarter, not harder.

Don't change your game for one course. If you visit a course with lots of elevated greens and you tend to hit the ball low, don't make a radical change trying to hit the ball high. It'll wreck your game for a week, at least. Play the game you have, accept whatever score you shoot, and move on. There are lots of courses out there, and the one with too many elevated greens isn't a good one. Don't let it goad you into changing.

It's amazing, the money these guys make playing the PGA Tour. It's good for them but bad for the fans, because the players don't need to play very often. They've got a lot, and they know most of the rest is going to the government anyway, so what's the use?

Would I do everything the same way? No. I'd find out more about what the game's about. Why does a ball fly differently out of wet grass than dry grass? Why doesn't the ball fly as far off a downhill lie as from a level lie?

To help me relax in the car, I listen to Tony Robbins CDs. I love the self-help stuff. My, what a head Tony Robbins has on his shoulders. He's a huge fan of my Natural Golf method. Maybe he'll let me go to one of his seminars.

Of today's players, I like Vijay Singh the best. I watch him and see how well he gets along with himself. He's not afraid to say what he believes. Of the women, Annika is the best, and for the same reason: She's at ease with herself. Watch her when she makes a bogey. She forgets it and goes to the next hole. She knows she's capable of birdying the next hole.

Hold the club in the palms, not the fingers. How do tennis players hold a tennis racket? In the palm. How do you hold a baseball bat? In the palms. Everyday items—an ax, a hammer—are held in the palms. They're the most sensitive parts of your body. Why would you want to hold a golf club in your fingers? It'll move all over the place!

At the LaBatt Open in 1955, I finished as second-low amateur. I always tried to give the people a show, teeing my ball on Coca-

Cola bottles, that sort of thing. When the tournament was over, Conn Smythe, the famous owner of the Toronto Maple Leafs, approached me. "What are you doing this winter?" he asked. "Going back to setting my pins," I said. "Well, I like a guy who has color," Mr. Smythe said. "You're too good to be setting pins." Mr. Smythe gave me $5,000 and sent me to Florida. He let me stay in his place at the Breakers.

At the 1956 Masters, I was on the practice range when Sam Snead came over. He gave me a forty-minute lesson, telling me to hit my irons like a fairway wood, meaning to sweep it instead of hitting down on it. I was in awe, and like a dumbbell proceeded to hit eight hundred balls. My right thumb swelled up so big I couldn't hit a ball without terrible pain. I played nine holes and quit. That was the last lesson I took, let me tell you.

I was getting ready to represent Canada in the 1956 Americas Cup in Mexico. I had my team jacket, got my inoculations, had my airline tickets. I was excited. I was the Canadian Amateur champion two years running, and I'd be playing against Harvie Ward, the U.S. Amateur champion two years running. Four days before I'm to leave, the Royal Canadian Golf Association convenes in a special meeting. From that, I received a letter telling me I wasn't a true amateur and to please return the jacket and airline tickets. I returned them. I wasn't an amateur by their definition, and I sure wasn't a pro. Where could I play golf?

In Canada, they like to keep people down. It's true. They can't stand seeing someone become successful, especially if they once were ahead of you. It eats at them, galls them more than they can stand; Canadians go out of their minds with jealousy and will do everything they can to drag you down.

Your mind is the generator, your body is the motor. The club is the trigger and the ball is a bullet. Take aim and fire!

With a titanium driver I'm hitting it farther now than when I was thirty-five, and that's the truth. It doesn't satisfy me—it bothers me. Do I want to hit the ball farther when I'm a hundred than I do now? No, it wouldn't be right. All anyone cares about is hitting it farther—even with the irons. Hitting the ball pure and accurate is more rewarding than hitting it far. Don't forget that, ever.

I've had my fill of competition and dislike traveling. But my game is holding up nicely. You know that show on the Golf Channel called *The Big Break*? I'd win that easily.

Sometimes you need ten more yards out of a drive. There's only one proper way to do that, and it's turning your shoulders more. It's the only way to keep your rhythm. Every other method—swinging faster or with more effort, changing your ball position, or anything else—will cost you accuracy. It has to. Otherwise, you'd swing that way every time.

I put 35,000 miles a year on my Cadillac. That's a lot because I drive slowly, never faster than sixty miles per hour. Why? I'm never in a hurry to get anywhere, and I get nervous driving any faster. I've gotten three tickets for driving too slowly, the last for going thirty-five in a fifty-mile-per-hour zone. The policeman also gave me a lecture, but like I told him, nobody is going to get me out of my comfort zone.

If you get nervous or afraid in tournaments or playing in front of other people, it's because you place too much value on it. You think the competition is more important than it really is. If you stand on the tee and feel like you're about to cross Niagara Falls on a high wire with no safety net, there's no way you'll have enough trust in yourself to pull it off. They say the only way to master that is through experience, and it's true, but all that means is getting to know yourself better. The better you get to know yourself, the more you'll like and trust that person inside. I won a lot of tournaments because I get along with myself real well.

To devalue the importance of competition, I count my money. It's not a bad idea to do it before you get out of your car to play golf. Make sure you have plenty in your pocket—I've carried $6,000 in cash just for this purpose—take it out and count all the bills. A round of golf important when I've got $6,000 in my pocket? Hah!

Fuzzy Zoeller

It's hard to see it at first glance, but Fuzzy Zoeller has changed. Once he was one of golf's more jocular entertainers, a lighthearted, come-what-may performer who never took winning or losing too seriously. All that changed one day at the Masters, when he spilled out a race-oriented line of repartee regarding Tiger Woods that was perceived as anything but funny. Zoeller protested that it was in jest, but the P.C. crowd turned him into a pariah, and it cut deeply. Today, back home in Indiana, Fuzzy outwardly is still the wisecracking, funny, ingratiating soul he always was, but just below the surface lurks a sadness and disillusionment that is hard for him to conceal.

What will never be hidden is his extraordinary skill as a golfer. He won the 1979 Masters, 1984 U.S. Open, and eight other PGA Tour events, and was a contender in majors several times. He had power and touch, both in golf and with people. Suffice it to say, there is nobody like him playing the tour today.

○ ○ ○

Being a tough competitor doesn't mean you have to be a jerk. My junior year of college, I played golf for the University of Houston. It was a national power, and the program was serious business. Early in the year, I was paired with an Oklahoma State player named Henry DeLozier, a good friend. On one hole Henry topped his tee shot. His second shot with a fairway wood stopped one foot from the hole. I said, "Nice shot, Henry," and that was a mistake. When we finished, our coach, Dave Williams, lectured me for ninety minutes on how my compliment "relaxed" Henry and helped him play well. I disagreed with that philosophy and kept saying "good shot" whenever I felt like it. We battled over that constantly, and it came down to either acting like a jerk to my fellow competitors or quitting the team. So I quit the team.

Maybe Dave Williams was right. I played in three Ryder Cups and was a pathetic match player. My record [1–8–1] is awful, and guys did seem to play well against me. In 1983, I had Seve Ballesteros all but beat playing the eighteenth hole. He was in a fairway bunker 240 yards from the green, and I'm sitting pretty. From that bunker, Seve hit a 3-wood onto the fringe of the green and made par to halve our match. Some people say it was the best shot in Ryder Cup history. What did I say to Seve? The same thing I told Henry DeLozier: "Nice shot."

Many of the younger players on the regular tour today are just plain shy. They started at an earlier age than I did and from day one really had the game hammered into them. They grew up more insulated from the outside world. So they're a little less comfortable around people. It shows in their interviews, their interaction with the fans, and even with each other. They just aren't people-oriented; caddies and teachers tend to get fired more often because of personality conflicts. I don't think they have as much fun as we did back in the 1970s and '80s. I have to say, I enjoyed the best years of the PGA Tour.

When I waved the towel at Greg Norman on the eighteenth hole at Winged Foot back in 1984 [the U.S. Open], I honestly thought I was done. I'd watched him one-putt four or five greens coming in, and that monster he made on eighteen, I thought it was for a birdie. I told my caddie, Mike Mazzeo, "That SOB is gonna beat us." There was no way I'm going to make a three, not where the pin was that day. Only when I was ready to hit did a USGA guy walk up and say, "You know that putt was for a par, right?" I said, "You're kidding. Where the hell did he hit his second shot?" He said, "He put it in the bleachers." I almost couldn't believe it; the bleachers are a good thirty yards to the right of the green. I felt like I was given new life. The eighteenth at Winged Foot is a bear, but par to tie came pretty easy.

After I holed out for par, a little kid—he couldn't have been older than twelve—said, "Mister, can I have that towel?" Without thinking, I gave it to him. I'm as nice as the next guy, but I've always regretted that. If you happen to see a grungy white towel hanging around, get it for me, will you?

I suppose you have to ask me about the Tiger incident at Augusta. Well, it's been terrible, the worst thing I've gone through in my entire life. What happened to me as a result? I got death threats against me, Diane, my kids. Even threats against the house. I received hundreds of terrible letters, almost all of them anonymous, and they're still coming—I got one this morning. It's been more than nine years now, and it still hasn't blown over. If people wanted me to feel the same hurt I projected on others, I'm here to tell you they got their way. I've cried many times. I've apologized countless times for words said in jest that just aren't a reflection of who I am. I have hundreds of friends, including people of color, who will attest to that. Still, I've come to terms with the fact that this incident will never, ever go away.

Everybody has a little idiosyncrasy in their swing. Mine is shoving the clubhead out beyond the ball just before I take the club away. When I was a kid, a pro over in Louisville named Moe Demling told me the best way to start the downswing is to feel the heel of the clubhead coming down first. That way you can't come over the top. The trouble was, I kept forgetting that little move. So Moe said, "Remind yourself by pushing the heel toward the ball." After hitting a million practice balls that way, I couldn't stop doing it, and I gave up trying forty years ago. I've made a career out of hooking every shot, sand wedges included. Versatile, I'm not. Effective, I am.

My dad was Frank Urban Zoeller. Everyone called him Fuzzy. When I came along and they gave me the same name, I took over Fuzzy and he became Frank. I never went by anything else. The last person to call me Frank was a nun when I was in first grade.

A couple of weeks into the school year, she called my parents to report that their son might have a hearing problem, because he didn't answer when she spoke to him.

High school basketball is a religion in Indiana, and where I grew up there were three high schools that were fierce rivals. There was Providence, Jeffersonville, and my school, New Albany. I played guard and was a pretty good sixth man. Not much on offense, but a nasty little defender. My junior year, we were playing Providence and I get called off the bench. In the first minute, I get the ball on a fast break and drive in for a layup. There's just one guy between me and the basket. He submarined me—took my legs out from under me. I did a three-quarter flip and landed on the back of my head. Worse, I tore the muscles all through my lower back. I still see the fellow who submarined me. Not long ago he told me that every time he read about me having a back operation—I've had three—he hurt, too. No hard feelings. Just part of sports.

The doctor said I'd have spine trouble when I got older, and was he ever right. It started in 1979 at the Memorial Tournament, where I did the worst thing a guy with a bad back can do: took my laundry to the dry cleaner. When I stepped out of the car, I turned my body a certain way and went straight to the ground. Couldn't move. Every heartbeat was agony. They got me to the hospital and shot me full of cortisone, which just caked up around the vertebrae and made it worse. It's pretty amazing I had the career I did after that.

Vodka does not ease back pain. But it does get your mind off it.

At a tournament a while back some players were carrying on about *The Daly Planet* on the Golf Channel and how disgusting it was. "If you don't like it, why don't you just turn the channel?" I asked them. I got no answer, because the truth is, they don't want to change the channel. They want to watch so they can criticize John for what he does on the show and take the Golf Channel to task for airing it. I say it's their right to air what they want, and if it annoys you, there's a good movie two channels over.

John Daly is not the only person who's had a drinking problem. He's not the only guy who's gambled too much or had troubled relationships. There are casinos in every city these days and bars on every corner, but you'd think he's the only human who's visited either one. It's his life, and he's living it the way he wants to live it. It's all his choice, and why can't we let it go at that? I'll tell you why: Because everybody's a critic.

People carry on about John's weight. But if the average person walked eighteen holes five days a week—that's thirty miles a week—and hit as many balls as he does, they'd be in trouble. John has no issues with strength. His stamina is good. John Daly, believe it or not, is in shape.

Before I made it to the PGA Tour, I played a mini tour in Savannah, Georgia. We played the Savannah Inn and Country Club for six straight weeks. We had a blast. The inn and the tour were run by Lou Rosanova, a wonderful guy who was affiliated with the Teamsters and, shall we say, "connected." Lou's great pride was the Dean Martin Room, a swanky nightclub deal at the inn.

One day some people from Hilton Head sailed their big yachts over to Savannah and partied at the inn. The party got out of hand, and the Hilton Head people tore up the Dean Martin Room. Lou never said a word, but you could tell he was angry. The next morning, we went down to the dock, and all you could see of those boats were the tops of the masts. Somehow they sank overnight. Only the Hilton Head yachts. Funny thing.

The Champions Tour's first full-field tournament of the year in 2003 was the Royal Caribbean Classic. I was asked to take a local TV reporter out on the course and give her a lesson. The tour approved it, and I was glad to do it. After the first round, a tour guy drove me out to the tee of the sixth hole, a par three, and I gave the reporter a lesson. They asked me to demonstrate by hitting a few shots, so, aiming sideways a couple of fairways over, I hit a few shots with the driver. While my caddie was picking up my balls, another official drives up. "What are you doing out here?" he asked.

"Doing this thing for the tour. Giving a lesson."

"Well, you can't practice on the course after the tournament has started. I'm afraid we'll have to disqualify you."

They had to do what they had to do, I guess. I understand the Rules of Golf. But the sponsor was furious, I felt bad because it was my first DQ ever on that tour, and two years later Royal Caribbean was out as the sponsor.

One thing about the mini tours, you never wanted to win by four or five shots. You wanted to manage your game so you won by only one shot, or two at the most. See, it was customary for the winner to pay the bar bill, and one year Bruce Lietzke ran away with a tournament and guys started drinking when he made the turn. By the

time he finished—the guys knew Bruce was going to win and got a two-hour head start—there was a five-hundred-dollar bar tab waiting for him. Bruce wasn't much of a drinker. I think he felt a little deflated.

When I design courses, I'm guided by the Diane Rule and the Career Day Rule. My wife, Diane, is an enthusiastic twenty-nine-handicapper who carries the ball about 130 yards. When I'm designing a hole with a carry over water or a bunker in front of the green, I ask myself, "Can Diane carry it?" If the answer is no, I'll do something to make it easier if I can, except from the championship tees, where the Diane Rule doesn't apply. The Career Day Rule is a little broader, but basically I want my course to be one where a fifteen-handicapper having a magical day can shoot 76. That can't happen when you put hazards and an automatic double bogey into play on ten holes. I don't design one-time-fling courses where the average guy pays $180, shoots 180, and never comes back. I don't build monuments.

Sam Snead was the best I ever saw. It's a fact. One day in the mid-'70s I was paired with Sam, and on one hole we both had 140 yards to the pin. I hit my standard 9-iron shot. Sam hit a little cut 6-iron that flew 135 yards, took one bounce, and stopped dead, stiff to the hole. The next hole was 170 yards, and Sam hit the 6-iron again, this time with a high, hard draw. I hit my standard shot with a 5-iron. See, when I hit a shot I had to go with my bread and butter. For Sam, any shot was his bread and butter. In my prime, I was pretty damned good—I did win two majors—but Sam at sixty-five was a better shotmaker than I ever was. When I picture a thirty-five-year-old Sam Snead, who was stronger and more powerful than the old version I played with, I see a golfer who had to be as good as anybody playing today, and far better than most.

People associate the yips with guys ramming three-foot putts six feet past the hole. But the yips in most cases are more subtle, and many tour players have had them. Hubert Green, for instance, had the yips four or five times during his career, and I'm talking his good years. He missed a million four-footers by burning the edges of the hole. To the average person his misses might have looked like misreads, but in fact it was his stroke. Paul Azinger has had them; why else would he switch to a belly putter?

At Savannah a few months ago, J.C. Snead had a fifty-yard shot to a green. He putted it and got up and down. I asked why on earth he chose his putter, and he said, "Have you seen me pitch lately?" Boy, I admired him for having the courage to use his putter in front of all those people. The yips aren't limited to the putter, no sir.

If the pressure is getting to you, whistle. In a barely audible way. It's the best way I know of to let go of tension. Music gets your mind off the situation, and the act of whistling melts the tension out of your body. I recommend something nice and rhythmic. Classic country and soft rock work for me. Jazz does not. It's hard to whistle jazz.

There's nothing wrong with choking. The trick is coming back after you choke, and not choking the second time.

I live on a farm, but I'm not a farmer. I drive three tractors, but I don't do anything with them except ride around. I own cows, but we don't milk them. I'll tell you, I'm glad I don't have to make a living farming. Too much hard work. Too many variables you don't have control over, like, is it going to rain? All I can say is God bless the real farmers out there.

Before a pro-am round one day, the practice green was crowded and all the holes were taken. So I stuck a tee in the ground and aimed at that. When I went out on the course the hole looked huge, and I made everything. It gave me the idea for a putting aid we call the Putting Peg. You stick it in the ground and putt at the peg instead of the hole. When the ball contacts the peg, it emits a sound like a ball falling in the cup. Sound in golf is very important—if you don't believe me, try hitting balls with earplugs in—and putting is no exception.

Getting the Putting Peg up and running was interesting. My business partner, Dave Lobeck, had a tough time trying to find the sound chip that caused the peg to make the noise. Dave wound up having some e-mail exchanges with several companies in China. They manufactured the chips, but none of them understood English very well. Dave wrote out the concept as best he could, emphasizing that battery life for the sound chip was crucial—the Putting Peg had to be built to last. A few days later, he gets an e-mail from one of the parties in Hong Kong.

"Battery life not matter," wrote the man.

Dave typed again why battery life was extremely important. A short time later, he gets another e-mail reply.

"Insist battery life not matter," it said.

Dave, frustrated, writes back that damn it, battery life absolutely does matter. A few days later, here comes the reply from Hong Kong.

"Ball on musical tee...club hit ball...tee explode.... Battery life not matter."

We went with another company.

I've always loved galleries, the bigger the better. I'm a people guy, but more than that is the way they frame the holes. When you're close to the lead and the fans are there in big numbers, all you can see is the fairway and the greens. You can't see the rough because that's where the people are. It's like they're with you, showing you the way, giving you a road map. The rough, forget it. You can't hit what you can't see.

When I'm playing badly, it's just the opposite. On every hole I'm reminded I'm not playing worth a damn, because the biggest part of the gallery is off with the leaders. And now the rough is exposed, it's right there saying, "I've been here for you all week; let's see you hit me again." It snowballs. I've never been known for going from worst to first.

A lot of amateurs are terrified of going up against a player who is clearly better than they are. They never play their best, because they aren't comfortable. There's one surefire way to get over that, and it's to ask yourself, "What if I beat him?" Imagine the possibility. Think of how much fun that would be. Think of the bragging rights, the pats on the back you'll get. The pressure is all on him. Relax and go after it. You've got nothing to lose.

"Don't sweat the small stuff" is pretty good advice. The problem is, "small" is subjective. Let me narrow it down for you: Don't worry about things they make more of.

I cut my teeth playing in gambling games around southern Indiana. I did okay right off the bat because the threat of losing money never worried me. When I turned pro, same thing—I never thought about the money. Why? Because every day at the U.S. Mint they're making more of it.

Most rich people got rich because they have big egos. Their ego drove them to be successful. So you can't blame them for wanting even more—they're just being themselves. I took another route to success: I was given a natural gift. No ego required. If I hadn't become a golfer, I doubt I'd be wealthy, because I don't have the sort of ego that drives a person all day long. I might have wound up driving a tractor.

I know a lot of good players come out of California, Florida, and Texas, but I still think climate is overrated. Winter never stopped us in Indiana. We played every day, even when it snowed. We played countless nine-hole rounds using a tennis ball and a 5-iron, which didn't hurt our games and probably helped.

Look at Arnold and look at Jack. One had a gift for touching people, the other had the gift of playing golf. Of the two, Arnold's gift was more powerful. My second year on tour, 1976, I was paired with Arnold, and the way fans embraced him was intimidating to me. I just hung back and watched, shot my 82 and got out of there. Arnold shot 73, but it was almost incidental in view of the way he mingled with the galleries. He was especially good with the very young and very old. There will never be anyone remotely like him again. We're in a different time.

The next time you fly, you'll notice that at some point most of the passengers are asleep. One reason is what else is there to do? The other reason is naps are the best thing in life. I feel my very best right when I walk off an airplane. Give me a twenty-five-minute nap and I'm good for the rest of the day.

Newspapers do a good job telling me what happened yesterday, but they'd be a lot more impressive if they could tell me what's going to happen tomorrow. The past doesn't interest me very much.

I started smoking when I was twenty-seven, which is pretty late to start a stupid habit like that. I had a golden opportunity to quit when I had my heart surgery. I went forty-five days without one, and then one night I was out having a drink with friends and lit one up. Halfway through that, I swore out loud, because I knew I was hooked all over again. You know, I have a theory that some people are just cut out for smoking. It tastes better to them, fits their personality, and is more apt to become a part of them than with other folks. I'm one of those people. I haven't even thought about quitting.

I live within thirty minutes of Churchill Downs. I was into quarter horses about twenty years ago, trailering them all over the country. But I got out of it. It cost me about $80,000 a year, which is a lot to pay for an occasional blue ribbon. It's a funny business. Everybody wants your good horses, nobody wants the bad ones, and all the horses eat the same and have the same vet bills.

Back in 1976, when I made eight birdies in a row at Quad City to tie the PGA Tour record, I wasn't the least bit apprehensive about trying to make it nine. Or ten or eleven. I guess that's sort of a gift, not being afraid to go low or do something unique. Most amateurs and even a lot of pros choke when they get a hot round going. Like I said, I'm not very interested in history. The birdie I just made was a thousand years ago. What can I do on the next hole?

When I got to the sudden-death playoff at the 1979 Masters, I couldn't have been more relaxed. It was my first Masters, and my only goal was to play well enough to come back the next year. With that in the bag, the playoff was pure gravy. Winning the Masters, believe it or not, for some reason felt incidental. When I missed a very makeable putt to win on the first playoff hole, I wasn't let down at all. And when I made it from six feet on the next hole to beat Ed Sneed and Tom Watson, I was as surprised as I was elated.

Ten years after I won the U.S. Open, I go up against Greg Norman again in the final round of the Players Championship. Now when a guy's on, he's on, and no amount of voodoo or hitting him in the shins is going to stop him. I shot twenty under par that week, maybe the best golf of my career, and he beat me by four. I mopped his brow with a towel on eighteen when it was over. I said "nice shot" a lot that day.

Hale Irwin is sixty-one, and he's still winning. He took the "window" theory, which said you had to get in your licks between fifty and fifty-eight, and blew it to smithereens. But I'm stubborn. I still believe in that magic window. Meaning, I'm just about done.

Byron Nelson

Visitors always knew what to expect from Byron Nelson, and during our visit at Los Colinas in Texas, he was his usual self: frank, insightful, and most of all, talkative. Though growing frail, Byron's voice was strong, his memory sharp, the range of the discussion broad. He drove himself to the club that day and ambled in using a cane. He was eager to start talking, and in our hour together he discussed not only golf, but chicken farming, woodworking, highway safety, religion, violent weather, his golf dreams, the importance of thrift, and the thing he was most proud of, his charity. This was one of several interviews I had with Byron over the years, and, as always, I left feeling uplifted and more than a little privileged to have been in his presence.

o o o

I stopped playing golf two years ago. I miss it very much. If I make it to heaven, I won't miss it anymore. There's no golf in heaven, but you don't mind, because you're so happy.

One reason I've lived so long is that I never dissipated. I never smoked, I never drank, and I never chased women. The other reason is heredity. Good genes are half the battle.

I never dreamed about golf when I was an active player. The dreams started after I quit. There was a pattern to them: They started out good and ended bad. I'd be at a tournament and leading, and I couldn't find my shoes. Or I couldn't find the entrance to the clubhouse. Or they'd be calling me to the first tee and I couldn't find my way there. If the dream got as far as me actually

teeing off, I'd need a certain club and it would be missing. I don't care who you ask, golf dreams are rarely good.

I never suffered a crushing defeat. If you play long enough, a terrible setback is bound to happen. It never did happen to me. The result is that people ask me about winning, not losing.

Experimenting with your swing is a lot of fun, and it can make you better. Just remember, it can also make you worse. It's okay to tinker, but don't stray too far from home.

People don't drive as safely now as they used to. All these freeways and boulevards have several lanes, with all the cars going in one direction. The drivers get complacent. Back in the 1930s and '40s, every road

had two-way traffic, and most of the lanes were pretty narrow. There were no concrete barriers. If you didn't pay attention every second, you could hit another car head-on, or veer into a ditch. I'm still a safe driver at age ninety-one. My eyesight and reflexes aren't quite as sharp, but I concentrate on what I'm doing.

PGA Tour golfers as a group are especially good drivers. Think of all the players, all the years, the millions of miles driven, and no terrible accidents or fatalities involving a tour player.... I don't count Ben Hogan. That wreck wasn't his fault.

In these troubled times, there are many people who haven't been religious who are thinking about joining a church. That can be confusing, because there are so many to choose from. My advice is to choose one that is active in the community. The doctrine is important, but helping people is sure to please the Lord.

Swing the club as though you were driving sixty miles an hour on the freeway. Not too fast, but not deathly slow. Once in a while, if the risk isn't great, you can push your swing to seventy, but never go faster than that. At my best I could go eighty on occasion, but that's too fast for the average golfer.

As movies go, you can't beat *The Sound of Music*. When Julie Andrews sings, it just lifts me up.

I didn't dip my knees on the downswing quite the way people thought I did. High-speed films show it was just an illusion. After impact, I tried to keep the club moving as low to the ground as possible. To do that I definitely dipped my knees. But that happened after I hit the ball, not before.

You'll be surprised how little wind will affect the ball if it's well-struck. That's something I impressed on Tom Watson, and he won five British Opens.

Check the texture of the skin on your hands. If it's a little dry or coarse like mine, you don't need a glove. Think how much money that'll save you.

The Byron Nelson tournament has raised seventy million dollars for charity. We raised more than six million dollars in 2001 alone, 11 percent of all the money raised on the whole PGA Tour. I talk on and on about that, but I can't help it. It's the greatest accomplishment of my life.

I love chickens. At one point I had 17,000 laying hens. They're so friendly once they get to know you. They'll gather at your feet and talk to you in a way you can almost understand. Not everybody thinks chickens are special, but I put them right behind horses as my favorite animal.

The best part of getting old is the way I'm treated wherever I go. I'm given more love now than I ever had in my life. I don't mean to brag, but I can honestly say I'm treated better than anybody I've ever known.

You ask how I can slaughter those chickens if I love them so much. Well, I'm not in that part of the business. My chickens lay eggs for me, and eventually I change them over. I sell them to somebody, and at that point my chickens…well, they just go.

Cows, on the other hand, are just cows. And I like beef.

Tom Watson

As interview subjects go, Watson was a surprisingly tough cookie. Certainly he had been interviewed by sportswriters a thousand times, and had written for *Golf Digest* for many years. But his work with the magazine always pertained to instruction and was performed solely with Nick Seitz, whom he knew and trusted. He didn't know me, and there were areas I wanted to take him where he did not want to go. Watson was every bit as cerebral as I'd been led to believe, and his observations and opinions were fresh and insightful. But I couldn't help feeling he played the round with only ten clubs when the rules for the interview allowed him all fourteen and a couple more. I left with the distinct impression that, to this day, nobody really knows Tom Watson.

○ ○ ○

From the time I won the Kansas City Match Play championship at age fourteen, I never wanted to be anything but a golfer. I found that I liked hitting good shots in front of people. I discovered that—at least when I swung the club—I had a little ham in me. That thrills me to this day, hitting shots that people can admire and wonder, *How did he do that?*

Golfers who play a lot of courses often encounter short ledges or retaining walls, and I always had fun hopping down from them. I could jump off something six feet high and land like a cat, no problem. Well, today I can't jump off anything higher than two feet without it just killing me. To realize it's going to be that way from now on...it isn't easy.

My first two years on tour I roomed with Ron Cerrudo and Bob Zender. Ron had won the Cajun Classic, and I asked him to tell me everything about it. I must have asked him to tell that story twenty times, and every time he told it, I sort of lived the experience along with him. Ron doesn't know it, but when I won my first tournament, the 1974 Western Open, his telling of that story did a lot for me. I almost felt I'd been there before.

I can still win a major. Things would have to go just right, but it can happen. The British Open this year is at Troon. Remember what happened there in 1982? I sure do.

Some guys have trouble sleeping the night before an important round. I never have. Invariably I sleep longer and better, and have more dreams, when I'm in contention and feeling pressure.

Not that all those dreams are good. I've had nightmares about golf. Who hasn't? I have two bad, recurring dreams. In one, I'm putting on a green that is cone-shaped, and the hole is at the top of the cone, so the ball either rolls back to my feet or goes past the crest and thirty feet away on the other side. In the other dream, I'm boxed in and don't have room to swing. Something vague is crowding me—the gallery maybe, or ropes, or something I can't pinpoint. I used to dream I was falling, which is the most common dream people have. That dream stopped. The golf dreams stayed.

A lot of amateurs who slice don't release the club well through impact. They don't "kill the pig." It's kind of a silly image, but picture a pig standing to your rear and to the left, adjacent to your left hip. You want to rotate the club to square at impact, then let it close even farther so that early in the follow-through you whack the pig in the head with the toe of the club. To kill the pig, you have to release the club. It's a nice little slice cure.

Did I have Jack Nicklaus's number? Let's see: I did get the better of Jack at the British Open in 1977, at the U.S. Open in 1982, and the Masters in 1981. But he finished first in majors eighteen times, and in the top three forty-six times. So did I have his number? The short answer—and it can't be any shorter—is no.

At the 1981 Ryder Cup, my swing was a mess. Jack was my foursomes partner, and when I drove I put him in the tall heather about four times. I asked Jack for a lesson, and one thing he said really stuck with

me: "As you get older your swing will get better." I thought, *Yeah, sure it will.* But Jack turned out to be right. These days my swing is much more rotary, or around, as opposed to upright. It's a more natural way to swing, easier on the body and every bit as sound. My ball flight is lower; I can't hit the fairway woods real high anymore, which is a bit of a drawback. But I'm much straighter and a better golfer from tee to green than I was twenty years ago.

In second grade I got sent to the principal's office every day for two weeks. A different reason every day. I'd finish my work ahead of the other kids and then have a terrible time sitting there doing nothing. The teacher, old Mrs. McKinley, didn't like me very much. I'm sure if Ritalin had been available somebody would have suggested I needed it. Thankfully it hadn't been invented yet, and somehow I turned out fine.

Bruce Edwards knew me so well. Whenever I got to feeling sorry for myself or started to get discouraged, Bruce would straighten me out. "Don't be a baby," he'd say, or "Let's stop moping and get with the program." I don't like being talked to that way, but when it came from Bruce I took it and usually responded to it. I've talked a lot about how Bruce made me better as a person, because I don't want to lose sight of the big picture. But he made me a better golfer, too. All those great years I had, all the success I enjoyed, was realized with Bruce by my side. How can I look back at all that and not love and miss him like a brother?

Growing up in Kansas City, I learned a healthy respect for lightning. A policeman friend of mine told me about encountering a lightning victim whose body inside was turned into something like Jell-O. At the

1975 U.S. Open at Medinah, I saw a flash of lightning and then heard the rumble of thunder within five seconds, which meant the lightning was less than a mile away. Nobody moved, but I said, "That's it. I'm invoking the lightning rule. I'm walking in." I was in the clubhouse for twenty minutes when P.J. Boatwright, the USGA's executive director, came in and said, "I need to talk to you." He had a problem, I think, with my walking in. I told him about the lightning, but P.J. seemed dubious. He said, "Let's go outside and just see about this lightning." We no sooner had stepped out the door when lightning struck right in front of us. The flash and boom were almost simultaneous. I didn't have to say another word, and the look on P.J.'s face told me he got the message.

Never saw a sport psychologist. Nothing wrong with them if they can help a guy deal with pressure. I never saw the need for one.

Many players on the senior tour wear magnets and copper bracelets, take herbal remedies and alternative medicines. Me, I'm a Vioxx and Advil guy. Nothing against that other stuff, but I'm from Missouri, the Show-Me State. When I see unequivocal proof that magnets work, I might give them a try.

Arnold Palmer, Jack Nicklaus, and Tom Watson have something very much in common: We don't look particularly good in clothes. When you have short legs and an average-size torso, you tend to look a little squatty. I try to look presentable, but my body's not conducive to looking like a model.

If you think of yourself as unlucky, you'll have bad luck. There's no scientific explana-tion for it, but it's a cold, hard truth in golf. That's one reason why bad bounces never bothered me as much as they did some people. The second you start thinking of yourself as a victim, you've had it.

Years ago the thinking was that we'd never see a really good tall golfer because of the problems they would supposedly have with leverage. I changed my mind about that after having lunch with Ben Hogan in 1985. I asked Mr. Hogan if the tall golfer stood a chance, and he said, "By all means." He was emphatic, and it so happens that most of the best players today—Woods, Els, Mick-elson, and so on—are over six feet tall. The day may come when we see someone six-foot-eight or even taller come along and just dominate. I wouldn't bet against it.

It's enough to say I'm religious. What church I go to is none of your business.

I don't need to go into detail as to why I quit drinking, other than to say it was becoming similar to driving a car way too fast. You can drive fast and get away with it, but the fact is, you're putting yourself in danger. So I just quit.

My favorite movie of all time is *Charly*. Cliff Robertson plays a man who is mentally handicapped. It was sad and funny, heart-breaking but uplifting. *One Flew Over the Cuckoo's Nest* is a close second.

I have lots of trophies and things, but my most prized possession is a dowry trunk that Byron Nelson made for my daughter, Meg. It's a beautiful piece of furniture, and to think Byron made it with his own hands makes it very special. Like I said, Meg has the dowry trunk. But it's still the most pre-cious thing anyone ever gave me.

A good conversationalist has the ability to say the right thing at the right time. He also recognizes the wrong thing to say and the wrong time to say it. I'm pretty good at saying the right thing, but I have a knack for saying the wrong thing. It stems from trying to be honest. Honesty can just be too painful.

If I could choose one player to win a Ryder Cup singles match for me, I'd take Larry Nelson. That surprises you, but Larry had a great record [9–3–1 in three Ryder Cups] and more than that, he was fearless. Larry saw some fighting in Vietnam, and that may explain why he couldn't be intimidated.

Everybody has choked. In the 1974 U.S. Open, I kept hitting the ball right to right. My nerves wouldn't allow me to adjust. That's what choking is—being so nervous you can't find a swing or a putting stroke you can trust, and gaining momentum from it. Byron gave me the best cure for it. Walk slowly, talk slowly, deliberately do everything more slowly than you normally do. It has a way of settling you down.

As a young man I enjoyed being around older people more than younger ones. I thought they had so much more to offer. I don't hang around older people as often these days. They're getting harder to find. Remember, I'm fifty-four.

Jim Thorpe

Golf is filled with unlikely heroes, and you can count Jim Thorpe among them. A self-taught hustler who came up the hard way, Thorpe had a very satisfactory PGA Tour career before finding gold on the Champions Tour, where he has won twelve times. He is remarkably unfazed by his growing up black in what was, in the 1960s, still a largely white game. Asked for a particular recollection of discrimination in golf, he shrugs and says he can't think of any.

Thorpe talks fast, swings fast, and thinks fast; there is an odd restlessness about him. He talks in a machine-gun cadence, often repeating the last word or phrase in a sentence for emphasis: "I put it right in the hole, baby, right in the hole." Thorpe is magnanimous and a bit elusive; attempts to reach him on his cell phone to follow up with his *My Shot* piece were unsuccessful. Said another tour player, "Big Jim doesn't like to cover the same ground twice."

o o o

Playing golf is just like handling a horse. A good groom or trainer can get up close to a horse and read him just right. He can tell if he's agitated or happy, fit or out of sorts, and most of all if the horse is prepared to give you his all.

Golf is the same way. There are days when the course and your golf swing are friendly and receptive to anything you want to try. There are other days when they're in no mood to be pressed. If you try to get too much out of the course or your swing, they rear up and bite you, kick you, or just buck you off. You can even damage your game, just like you can damage a horse. On days like that you don't want to give up, but you definitely have to settle for something less than you might like.

I don't go to the track to lose money. Over the years I've done fine. It isn't that complicated, really. You look at how the horses are trending, who the trainers are, the condition of the tracks they've been running, the distances they run at, and the types of races they like to run. You narrow it down to four or five horses, and from there it's like deciding between a 5- and 6-iron. Meaning, you go with your gut.

What happened to make old Thorpy turn it all around? My whole career on the PGA Tour, all I cared about was the ten inches just before impact. I knew if I could make my clubhead get to square in that short little space, I could make money. It worked pretty well. Then, just before I turned fifty, a light came on. I doubled that strip to twenty inches, taking into account the ten inches after impact. I started hitting through the ball instead of at it. That's when I started playing the best golf of my life. If there's a secret to playing this game, it's to just let the ball get in the way of the clubhead.

When I was forty-eight, I was invited to play in a tournament for high rollers at Foxwoods [Resort Casino] in Connecticut. Carol and I drove down from Buffalo, and while I was on the range, it started pouring rain. The tournament was washed out, but instead of going into the casino—I was too broke to gamble—I stayed out there hitting balls. The only people on the range were me and this little chubby boy at the other end. I wandered over and gave him a little help with his swing. Showed him the right grip and stuff. After we'd finished, Carol and I drove back to Buffalo. When we got home the phone rang. It was a lady from Foxwoods saying Mr. Kenny Reels would like you to come down and have dinner with him the next day. I didn't know who the man was, but I said okay, and we drove back down.

When Kenny Reels arrived, it was like the Red Sea parted for him. It turned out he was the chief of the Indian tribe that owns the casino. He shook my hand and said, "I want to thank you for spending time with my son on the range. The only thing he's talked about since is how he met Jim Thorpe of the PGA Tour." And then he asked if I'd be interested in representing the casino, and would I put together a proposal and send it to him. I agreed, but I left the

money part blank. I had no idea what to write in there, but in truth I would have taken it for $3,000 because we were broke.

Kenny called, noted that I hadn't written in a figure, and asked if I'd like him to fill it in for me. He said, "If you like it, fine; if not, good luck to you." When the proposal came back, he'd written in $100,000. I had it back in the mail to him faster than you can say Jack Robinson, and the rest is history. It's turned out to be a deal that, at the time, pretty much saved my life. Strokes of luck like that make a man think, you know?

The most nerve-racking moment for most golfers is on the first tee at the start of an important round. The first time I played with Arnold Palmer, I literally could not get my ball to stay on the tee, and knowing he was watching me just made it worse. So here's what you do to fight first-tee jitters: Always hit first if you can. I used to pray for that. That way you can sneak up to the tee and put the ball on the peg while nobody's watching.

No moment I've had in golf can match the fear and nervousness I feel when I go to a championship prize fight. All that tension that's in the air beforehand; it's just about more than Big Jim can handle. I get sick to my stomach, but I can't tear my eyes off it. The night Mike Tyson fought Larry Holmes, I was only a few rows back from ringside. When the fight got under way, I thought I was gonna die. I knew Tyson was going to knock Holmes out, and the anticipation of that frightened me something fierce. Sure enough, Tyson landed a big left hook to Holmes's head, and this huge halo of sweat flies so far in my direction I couldn't get my cigar lit. I mean, I was scared. Golf can't hold a candle to that, baby.

I'm on the first tee in the final round of the 2001 Senior PGA Championship in New Jersey. I'm tied for the lead with Tom Watson and Bob Gilder, and I'm spitting cotton. When the starter introduces me, he says, "Now on the tee…from Heathrow, Florida…please welcome…Jim Dent." There was some nervous laughter when he said that, except from Watson, who thought it was just plain funny. When the poor guy realizes his mistake, I can tell he just wants to die. So I kind of mutter so people can hear, "Why the hell couldn't he say Tiger Woods?" That made everybody laugh like crazy, and it relaxed me enough to where I could play my best. Watson got me by a shot that day, but the point is, the best way to ease tension is to laugh.

At New Orleans one year in the 1970s, I was on the range taking a break between bags of balls. I was watching Tom Weiskopf, Lee Trevino, and some other top players hitting balls and listening to them talk it up between shots. They were laughing and having a great time. Just then Jack Nicklaus walked onto the range with his caddie, Angelo [Argea]. Trevino calls out, "Jack, nice to see ya! Come over here and hit a few with us." Jack gave them all that little smirk of his and said, "Actually, Lee, I'm here to win this week." He kept walking to the other end of the practice tee and started practicing by himself. Man, those guys got real quiet. They all started paying attention to what they were doing. If ever there was a moment that proved who the best player was—and why—that was it.

A brand-new golf ball has always been a wonderful thing to me. Still is. I love just taking them out of the package. We hunted for balls when I was a kid, and finding one that was almost new was a big thing. Even

into my twenties, new balls were sometimes hard to come by. It never left me, and today the biggest proof that I'm wealthy lies in the fact that I get all the new balls I want for free. When I pass them out to friends, I feel like a king. Guys my age are suckers for new balls; if you want to give somebody in their fifties a Christmas present they'll really appreciate, spring for a dozen.

The first hole at Alaqua Country Club in Longwood, Florida, is a dogleg-left par 5 with water down the left side. If you hit a big hook over the corner of the water you can reach the green easy with your second shot. In the pickup game I play in there, we all hit two balls off the first tee. And that first shot, I always hit a low one that starts out to the right and then runs around the corner. My partners say, "Big Jim, why don't you just bomb it over the corner on the fly? That's nothing for you." And I have to tell them, "I can't risk hitting that new ball into the water, man."

Not long after we moved to Florida, I found a church: Crossings Community Church, over in Lake Mary. When I met the pastor, Keith Wilkins, I was drawn to him and knew this was the church for me. I did a little to help the church financially, but then a successful guy on the board, Mike Lewis, suggested we try to do something really significant. I thought about it and prayed some, and finally told the congregation I'd donate $250,000. I'd have to do it over a three-year period—I'm not that rich.

I hadn't done much to that point last year and wasn't playing very well, but two weeks later I went to Austin, and before I played I told God to let me have a good week so I could do something for my church. Standing on the first tee, it was like something happened to me inside, because

I played like a man on fire. I was right there after two rounds, and Sunday morning I read in the paper that first place paid $247,500. That sent chills down my back.

The last round was just a formality. I shot 68, won the tournament, and signed over the whole thing to Pastor Keith. Everything they needed—the baptismal pool, a van, new seats for the sanctuary that weren't rock hard—between Mike Lewis and me, we covered it. The following week, I won again. And this was like God saying, "See? You did the right thing." But I'll tell you, I wasn't off the course long before Carol got in touch with me. "Don't get crazy, now, baby," she said. "You've got kids and a wife to think about, too." So that one stayed with us.

I was in the clubhouse tied for the lead at the Long Island Classic in 2004. The TV cameras are on me while I'm waiting for Bobby Wadkins to finish the eighteenth hole. He's got a putt for par to stay tied with me, and before he hits it, the camera pans over to me. I give a thumbs-down sign. A few people didn't think that was good sportsmanship, but give me a break. You think I'm gonna sit there and say, "C'mon, Bobby, make the putt"? You think I'm gonna sit there and not think anything? You gotta be crazy. Of course I want him to miss. I like him, and he's a nice guy, but I want to win the tournament, man. It's my business.

If I had it to do over again, I'd cut the time I spent practicing my long game in half. I'd spend it around the practice green chipping and putting like I do now. Over and over again, I see tournaments decided by the guy who makes the crucial up-and-down at the end. The short game is where the money is, especially for you amateurs.

Vijay Singh came to the PGA Tour when I was finishing up. This was in 1993 and '94. We became close friends. You know, I never saw a guy work harder on his game than he did. But he didn't practice like he was in a hurry to get somewhere. He was just out there all day, every day, calmly working away like he knew it was going to pay off. Watching him, I remembered a passage from the Bible my mother used to repeat to us all the time: "But many that are first shall be last; and the last shall be first." It takes a while, but persistence always pays off.

Vijay and I spent our free time sitting around my house. One day he picked up an old copy of *Golf Digest* and was looking at some stats. "Jim, it says here your first-place check for winning the Milwaukee Open in 1985 was $54,000. Man, that's chump change. I make that just for showing up."

I told Vijay that hurt and to lighten up, that times were hard just now, and I didn't think it was funny. He said "Of course, Jim. I'm sorry, I didn't realize." He puts down the issue, but in a few minutes he picks up another one.

"Jim, did you know that I get more money for winning one tournament now than you did the whole year in 1985, when you were fourth on the money list?"

"What's your point, Vijay? You think that's funny?"

"I'm sorry, Jim. I forgot. Please forgive me, I wasn't thinking."

Two minutes later, with no magazine to look at, he says, "By the way, Jim, did you know that I get more in one month from my equipment deal than you did the entire..."

I wanted to kill that man. When you hear Vijay's buddies say on TV that Vijay in private has a wonderful sense of humor, this is what they're talking about.

I grew up next to a golf course in Roxboro, North Carolina. My dad was the green-keeper there for fifty-six years. At that golf course, in this little pocket of the world, there was no racism, no prejudice. It existed elsewhere, but not there. The people treated my father and his kids—there were twelve of us—with respect. So I grew up treating people the way I wanted to be treated, and almost always people sensed that and treated me well in return.

Now, many African Americans didn't have my experience, and as a result they became insecure. And what they continue to see as race issues really are personal issues stemming from that insecurity. There comes a time when you have to stop blaming others for your problems and start digging a successful life out of the ground like everyone else. It's there for you. Just do it. There's a place for welfare in America, but not as a way of life. If a person gets an education—and in this country an education is there for everyone—you can make it happen. I'm proof of that.

It really bothers me to know there were more black players on the tour in the late 1960s and early '70s than there are today. It's mind-boggling because, if anything, there's more opportunity now than when I came up. The loss of caddie programs, competition with other sports, and not enough First Tee outlets hurt, but you know what it comes down to? Golf isn't cool. You can tell kids it's cool, but when they pick up the game it isn't long before they find there's nothing cool about going out in ninety-degree heat and hitting 3-iron shots until your hands bleed. There's nothing cool about spending all that time by yourself playing and practicing. What's cool about spending what few bucks you have on equipment, green fees, and getting to and from the course? Golf can be fun, but getting real good at it is less "cool" than it is hard, back-breaking work.

When Tiger Woods drives into the rough, he has a wedge left for his second shot. When I drive into the rough, I still have 175 yards to go, and 5-irons and tall grass aren't a good mix. Drive it straight! Never hit your driver with more than 80 percent of your power.

Whatever the worst part of your game is starting out, you'll probably fight that thing your whole life. I've seen it time and again in golf, and it was true with me until about 1986. I'd always been a poor driver of the ball because I rotated the clubface from open to square through impact. But after I had wrist surgery, I couldn't rotate the club anymore. I was forced to block the ball through impact, and as a result I started driving the ball a lot straighter.

One time I bought a thoroughbred horse named Happy Visitor. The guy I bought him from said his legs were a little sore, and when I took him to the vet to be checked out, the vet said his legs were even worse than the seller had said. On the outside, Happy Visitor looked to be washed up, but I had a feeling about him. I fed him well and rested him a long time before putting him back on the track, and when he became sound he reminded me of Gary Player. He wasn't big, and his form wasn't much, but he had a huge heart. Happy Visitor changed my outlook on golf. He took away all the worries I had about my technique and the fear I had about my swing not holding up under pressure. That horse taught me that golf is 90 percent heart.

Stay away from trifectas and perfectas. Unless you're damn good, don't do tri-keys, where you pick one horse to win and a couple of other horses to place, and show, in any order. Unless you're a serious player, pick one horse to win, place, or show. And don't bet the ranch. Winning is sweet, but losing more than you can afford is a downer.

Three rules for the casino: (1) Bring cash only; leave the credit cards at home. (2) Forget what they say about slot machines having the worst odds. That's true, but they're fun and they pay the biggest premiums when you do hit. (3) Pick an amount you're gonna quit at when you get ahead, and pick the maximum amount you'll lose. Never violate those rules.

If I were in charge of the NBA, the NFL, or Major League Baseball, I'd do one thing that overnight would make the players give their best effort every single day, and make every day of the season real dramatic. I'd make all the salaries performance-based and limit all contracts to one year. If they argued that it was too much like the PGA Tour—meaning too tough—I'd come right back and remind them that, unlike tour players, they get half the year off.

Tiger is one tough kid. Having a family is going to affect him, just like it did Nicklaus. It's going to make him even more serious, make him even better. But you know what? I don't think he's gonna get Jack's record [twenty major championships]. Tiger has elevated the game of every player out there, and they're all gonna get better yet. There are some kids you haven't heard of who are going to be giving him fits five years from now. What wisdom I've got tells me he isn't going to get there.

Little kids today don't know how to go outside and play. My brothers and I used to cut the limbs off of dogwood trees and shape them into golf clubs. Then we'd wrap these acornlike things that fell from the trees in aluminum foil. You hit them about thirty yards. My four brothers and me had some great duels with those things.

You know the surest sign that somebody grew up spoiled with a silver spoon in their mouth? When they hit a brand-new ball into the woods and don't bother looking for it. That disgusts me. It shows a wastefulness and lack of respect for what they have that's hard to put into words. Half the time, I'll go into the woods and look for that ball for them. If I find it, I make a point when I give it back to the guy: "Here's your brand-new ball, man," I'll say and sort of slam it into their hand. Most of the time they don't know what's eating me.

The way life is today, you can't discipline teenage girls the way my sisters were punished when I was a kid. Physical punishment is out, of course. Grounding them doesn't work, because if there's a TV or the Internet in the house, grounding them is like rewarding them. You know what works better than anything? Take away their cell phone for a week. I never saw my daughters so upset as when my wife took away their phones. You'd have thought we'd banished them to a desert island. When they got their phones back, they were like angels for a long, long time.

A guy was arguing to me once how every young person in America would really benefit from compulsory military service. He said the discipline, the self-reliance, the respect they learn to show others is amazing. He asked if I'd ever served, and did I agree with him, and I said yes and yes. I didn't tell him that I'd been discharged after six weeks because I had asthma. I just kept agreeing with him. Heck, the Army turned my late brother Elbert Jr. into a perfect gentleman. It still sounds like a good idea.

The best golfer I ever played with was Greg Norman. Period, end of story. He really had a more complete game than Nicklaus. But under stress, Greg's thinking became clouded. He definitely had some rotten-ass luck, but he also went at too many flags, pulled the wrong club, tried the wrong kind of shot, all kinds of things. I'm not the smartest guy in the world, but even watching him on TV I'd say out loud, "What are you doing, man?" If he had a *Nicklaus* on his bag, he probably would have won ten majors.

Remember when Norman lost to Nick Faldo at Augusta ten years ago? I was in the gallery that day. I wasn't in the field, but I go there every year. Let me tell you, the key to that day was Norman's tee shot at the twelfth. He hit it at the flag on the right, came up short, and went in the water. But if his ball had carried less than a foot farther, he would have been stiff. That one foot was the difference between a two and five, and if he'd made the birdie there, it would have given him a huge lift, and he would have brought it home. But it didn't happen. Poor Greg. At least he had the guts to keep coming back.

A lot of guys in my spot will look back on their life and career and say, "I'd do it all over again." Not me, man. There were a lot of years of scratching around, hustling, doing a few things wrong and a few right, of hanging out at the racetrack, at the craps tables, living hand to mouth at times.

Lots of harrowing stuff. It was fun, but I wouldn't do it again. Now if I feel that way, how about Carol? I married her when I was twenty-nine, and she was pretty brave, buying a ticket to win on me. She never let go of it, even during the times when I was bringing up the rear. She raised two fantastic daughters and kept steering me toward the straight and narrow, which I've yet to find. She's just an angel, straight out.

I had three wins on the PGA Tour, two of them at the Seiko-Tucson Match Play. It was the only match-play tournament every year on tour at the time, and I got it twice. That tournament brought out the hustler in me. I'd give guys the lip a little bit, which they aren't accustomed to at the pro level, and I'd do a little gamesmanship. Against Jack Renner in the final one year, he hit a driver off the first tee, and I just blistered a 1-iron. I stopped at the short ball in the fairway and said to my caddie—so Jack could hear—"This has to be my ball; I only hit a 1-iron." That got inside his head a little, and I handled him fine.

The next year, I went up against Tim Simpson, who was just a fantastic ball striker. All day I told him what a wonderful ball striker he was, and all day he hit it inside me. But he couldn't make a putt to save his life, I beat him easily, and my remarks about his ball striking had a lot to do with that. You know something? If I were in that WGC Match Play deal, I could beat some people.

You want to beat me? Take me to a course with lots of water. I'll play chicken, because I can't stand to risk hitting a new ball into a water hazard. It's like throwing money away, man. Even playing for a hundred dollars a hole, I can't make myself take a chance of losing a four-dollar ball.

Bob Toski

Bob Toski is the most influential teacher of the last fifty years. That is a bold statement and difficult to justify in that, unlike many who followed him, he did not elect to teach great tour players exclusively. His heart always was in helping the everyday amateur improve. Nobody did it more effectively than "Toss," who was dean of instruction with the *Golf Digest* Instruction Schools for many years and authored scores of articles and several books that helped him achieve that end. Still, he widened the knowledge base of his profession and provided important frames of reference. He also was an exceptionally fine player, leading the PGA Tour money list in 1954.

To meet with Bob at length is to get the full measure of his charismatic personality. He will be gruff and profane, gentle and cajoling, verbal and physical all in the course of an hour. His energy level is profound, and his genius for golf tends to outrun his vocabulary; his language is filled with non sequiturs, mixed metaphors, and run-on sentences that can be difficult to track. His thoughts on learning and teaching golf, and his own extraordinary life, made for an exceptional chapter in the *My Shot* series.

o o o

A firm handshake doesn't reveal a thing about character. All it tells me is, you're probably going to hold the club too tight.

I entered a tournament under my given name, Bob Algustoski. It was a big moment for me. On the first tee the announcer boomed out, "Now playing, Bob Aglus...Aguss...oh, hell, play away." The gallery roared. From then on, I was Bob Toski.

My best year on the PGA Tour was 1954. I won four tournaments and was the leading money-winner. I weighed 118 pounds. The moral is, if you're good enough, you're big enough.

Swinging a weighted practice club will do more for your swing than a hundred swing-training gizmos combined.

I've yet to see a golfer who wasn't disappointed when he saw his swing on video for the first time.

I never played in the British Open, because in 1953, first prize was about $1,500. You couldn't cover expenses, even if you won. The history and tradition of the Open are wonderful, but it never surpassed the need to feed and clothe my wife and kids.

We all have "natural" swings. The problem is, a natural swing produces a slice. That's because the homunculus, the part of the brain that controls motor movement, sees the hands as the largest part of your anatomy. When you're a baby you're constantly moving your hands away from your body so you can explore things in your environment. Now, when the day comes to play golf, the instinct to move your hands away from you really takes over. On the downswing the hands move away from the body too soon, out toward the target line, and you end up cutting across the ball from out to in.

Thanks to the homunculus, I make a very good living.

I love competition. If you know someone my age or older you think can beat me, come on down to Florida, name the stakes and let's tee it up. I'm the best seventy-five-year-old golfer in the world, with the possible exception of Joe Jimenez.

I won a penmanship contest in grade school. The principle is the same as golf: Your right palm faces down with the thumb and forefinger touching. And you move the pen with your entire arm, not just the wrist.

Somewhere there's a ten-year-old kid practicing with some version of the long putter. When he grows up, he'll putt better than anyone the world has ever seen.

People sing in the shower because they sound better in there. You get that little echo off the walls. I may be the best shower singer of all time. When I belt out "How Great Thou Art," I believe God is pleased by the expression of praise and talent coming from the Toski bathroom.

God can hear me longer, now that I have a thirty-gallon water tank.

It's better to play than to practice.

If your back hurts from playing golf, you're not swinging correctly. If you shift your weight to the left on the downswing, and let your right heel come off the ground, you should be able to play forever.

As a ball striker, Ben Hogan was every bit as great as people say he was. But Tiger Woods is much, much better than Hogan ever was.

Everything about golf is better today, except the sounds. The click of a persimmon driver striking one of those soft balata balls and the sound of steel spikes clattering across the parking lot were heavenly. The *plink* of titanium does nothing for me.

Many old people take pride in saying they live in the present and think only of the future. They must have had a miserable past. I think of the old days all the time. I had a dream about Sam Snead the other night. I also dreamed about my mother, who died when I was six. I saw her face; it was very comforting. I'm a very nostalgic person.

A teacher can get a lot of attention working with tour players, but the challenge isn't that great. What's hard is taking someone who is totally spastic and turning them into a ten-handicapper.

Boca Raton is the road-rage capital of America. Half the population is eighty years old and drives fifteen miles an hour under the speed limit. The other half consists of twenty-year-olds who think they're the reincarnation of Dale Earnhardt. You put those two groups on wide, flat, well-paved roads, and you've got something you could charge admission to see.

Men, your wife appreciates that you are a better golfer than she is. She also suspects you don't understand the golf swing as well as you think you do, and she's right. So, for the sake of world peace, keep your advice to yourself.

I've never been asked to refund money for a lesson. Please don't start now.

David Graham

In his glory years in the 1970s and '80s, David Graham was a hard-edged character, irredeemably stubborn, blunt, and dogmatic. It was easy to see why: His early life in his native Australia was filled with emotional rejection, financial desperation, and a golf game that just wasn't good enough to make it. With the possible exception of Ben Hogan, Graham went through more to succeed than any golfer I've known, overcoming a lack of raw talent with guts and determination. His linear, precise game eventually helped him win the 1979 PGA Championship and 1981 U.S. Open.

After he turned fifty and joined the Champions Tour, Graham softened. And when he developed a severe heart problem in 2005 that drove him from the tour to his home in Montana, he softened even more. In my two days with David, he drove us everywhere, picked up every check, opened his home, and spoke lovingly of his family and friends. He cried and laughed often, sometimes both at once. He is a complicated man, but one whom it is impossible not to respect, admire, and like.

○ ○ ○

It's been twenty-five years since I won the U.S. Open at Merion, and it's a good thing they have video, because I can hardly remember a thing about the final round. I was in a daze, in the zone. The details—every fairway hit except the first, a hole I birdied; every green hit except landing on the collars at number nine and number eleven, leaving me twenty-five feet from the hole at most—were a blur until it was over. In fact, the only clear memory is a bad one, my three-putt at the fifth hole. Isn't that odd? Some people felt the 67 I shot was the best closing round ever in a U.S. Open. Well, it would be nice if I could have seen it.

In 1996, Merion invited me to its hundredth anniversary. It was called Merion Cricket Club well before they opened the golf course there in 1912. Anyway, after the golf, the membership gathered around the eighteenth green. As a band played, they had me walk from the eighteenth tee down the fairway, up and over the hill. When I appeared, they gave me the most wonderful applause I've ever heard. It was like coming home, really. My most thrilling day happened at Merion. The most heartwarming day happened there, too. And I'm glad to say I remember everything about it.

A couple of summers ago I developed a cough. I was at a tournament in Boston and figured I'd just play through it. I didn't feel much better on Saturday but played anyway, coughing all day. On Sunday I felt even worse. On the eighth green my caddie looked at me and said, "Boss, you look awful. You've got to go in." I told him, "I think I'll just hit this putt." I stood over the ball and collapsed. They got me to the hospital, and I wound up spending five days there. It was congestive heart failure, cardiomyopathy, and one or two other things. The big muscles and small muscles of my heart don't work well together, and there's nothing that can be done except to give me lots of pills to manage it. That was the end of me as a golfer. It was almost the end of me, period.

Early in my career, I had a three-quarter backswing. I just wasn't comfortable taking the club back to parallel. In 1978, on the advice of Gary Player, I began swinging a weighted driver. I drilled big holes in a persimmon clubhead and poured hot lead into the holes, then poured more lead down the shaft till it was brimming. After it cooled, I put a new grip on. This club stretched out my swing very nicely. I liked it so much that I took to actually hitting balls with it. That summer I swung the club back to parallel for the first time and played great golf. To this day, even with all the practice devices that are available, I don't think there's anything better for your swing than a simple weighted club.

I was never much of a showman. I was too scared. No matter how big a lead I had, I could never punch the air with my fist after, say, a birdie at the seventeenth. Because in the back of my mind, I was aware that I could double bogey the eighteenth hole and bring about the most embarrassing situation of my life. Emotionally, I preferred to keep my cards close to my vest.

It was a good move on my part. In 1979, I came to the last hole of the PGA Championship at Oakland Hills with a two-stroke lead. One of the golf magazines—it wasn't yours—had offered $50,000 to anyone who broke the PGA seventy-two-hole scoring record, and another $50,000 if he broke the eighteen-hole record. A par would have given me a 63 and the first record; a birdie would have given me both. Well, I blocked my drive well to the right, and although I had an open shot, there were too many people about to figure my yardage. So I asked my caddie, Willie Peterson—you remember Willie, he was Jack Nicklaus's caddie at Augusta for years—to get a yardage. Willie's answer was shocking: "You haven't asked me one question all the way around. I don't know. Figure it out yourself." I said, "Excuse me?" Willie just clammed up.

I ended up guessing the yardage and hit a 6-iron dead on line but over the green. I chili-dipped the chip shot, then chipped up and missed the putt. I made a double bogey, and the next minute I'm in a sudden-death playoff against Ben Crenshaw. Walking up to the scorer's tent, Willie says, "Don't worry, Boss, we'll get 'em in the playoff." I said, "Don't even speak to me. The farther you stay away from me, the happier I'll be. Just carry the clubs."

Frankly, I don't know how I got from the scorer's tent to the first tee. Ben hits a beautiful drive, and I hit a duck hook. I chipped out a hundred yards short of the green, then hit a wedge shot about twenty feet to the right of the hole. And then I made the putt. And on the second hole I made a ten-footer to tie him again. Finally I won on the third hole with a birdie.

Standing over that twenty-footer on the first hole, I had no inkling I would make the putt. You talk about players willing the ball into the hole? Well, my will and composure were shot. I can only conclude that a higher power was in control that day.

If I'd lost that tournament, it probably would have been the end of David Graham the golfer. There's a good chance I would have gone home and thought myself a choker for the rest of my career. Can you think of another instance where a guy blew a two-shot lead on the last hole and then won the playoff? It just never happens, but that day it happened to me.

Jack Nicklaus preferred leather grips on his clubs. So did a few other guys, but Jack's grips were different. He liked the grips to get old so the leather was rock hard and shiny. They were slick as glass. Whenever I swung one, it almost flew out of my hands—and I had strong hands! If you hit a ball out on the toe of those small MacGregor irons, it would sting your hands something awful. Jack has small hands that weren't particularly strong, and how he played in the rain is anybody's guess. I suppose his grip pressure in every finger was absolutely perfect, and he had to accelerate the club very purely just to hold on to the club. That's one mystery Jack will take to his grave. "I love 'em like that," he'd say, then change the subject.

Can you imagine seeing Jack Nicklaus today lighting a cigarette during an interview? Or Arnold Palmer? It's almost unimaginable that these men ever smoked, yet they did. And so did I, until five years ago. Even then, I replaced the cigarettes with cigars for a while. In terms of difficulty, quitting was about as easy as winning the U.S. Open.

For years, Jack would invite me to Augusta National for practice rounds the Tuesday, Wednesday, and Thursday the week before the Masters, and I used it to pick his brain. I asked him once why he made such a long backswing—his shoulder turn was second to none. Jack thought for a minute and said, "Good shots are worth waiting for."

It's one day at a time now. I have good days and bad. I can't walk uphill at all. Sometimes fifty yards is an ordeal. It's not totally debilitating. I can still travel some. I shoot skeet, go to dinner with friends, and have people over. I have a good life.

The friendships I've made in Montana are much different than the friendships I had on tour. For the first time, they're not founded on or built around golf, and that's made it very challenging for me. Golf comes up in conversations, sure, because it's been my life. But we talk far more about the gun club, the goings on around Whitefish and Kalispell, all sorts of things I wasn't aware of before. Forming these new friendships is like learning to walk, because they're rooted in everyday lives that cover the gamut. It's required a higher level of consideration, loyalty, trust, honesty, and thoughtfulness. I've had to work very hard at that, because so many of the friendships I have in pro golf are more like acquaintances because of the transient life we all led.

Hand me another Kleenex, will you? I cry a lot these days. My wife, Maureen, says it's a side effect from the handful of pills I take for my heart every day, but I'll admit I've become very sensitive, a baby really. All my life I fought like the devil to be successful, to escape the terrible start I had in life and build a good life for my wife and children.

I pushed all the time, and one day I almost died and missed the things I'd worked for. All the goodness has hit me all at once. Every time I turn around, I'm living the end of a really happy movie.

After I got sick, I spent six months feeling sorry for myself. You know, the "why me?" syndrome. Then I stumbled across a TV program about St. Jude Children's Hospital. They're talking to a five-year-old girl with cancer. She said, "I can choose to be sick and unhappy, or I can choose to be sick and happy. I choose to be happy. It's a personal choice." That was the end of Mr. Graham feeling sorry for himself. Hand me that Kleenex again.

After I got sick, a year went by without me so much as lifting a club. Then a friend needed a partner for the big member-member at Iron Horse here in Whitefish. They let me play, using a cart with no restrictions. The problem was, I had to play off scratch. My opening tee shot, I hit four inches behind the ball and sent it eighty yards. Embarrassing. On the fourth hole, a par 5, we were forty yards short of the green in two and made an eleven. On the seventh hole, a par 3, I shanked a ball into the woods. We were well down the list, but the next day we shot ten under and had a nice time. The upshot of that experience is that I haven't hit a ball since. Gave all of my clubs away except the irons I used to win the PGA and the U.S. Open, and the Bulls Eye putter I used at Merion. Threw fifteen pairs of golf shoes in the dump. I'll never play again. Too embarrassing.

That shank, by the way, was the first one I ever hit in my entire life. I'm serious. I just cannot remember ever hitting one. Man, was it embarrassing. Now I understand what all the commotion is about.

I hated school and quit to turn pro when I was fourteen in Australia. My father, who was a nasty guy and lived in a separate part of the house from my mother, said he'd never speak to me again if I chose that route, and boy, he meant it. I left home when I was sixteen, and years of desperation followed. No money, a terrible golf game, no friends, no education, terribly insecure. I'd mark six-inch putts in the small pro tournaments I played in and would hold up the whole course because the thought of blowing a putt and losing the few dollars was too dire to consider.

Anyway, when I came to America in 1969, I wasn't much different from the immigrants who came here a hundred years ago. I had nothing except desire and a trade, and the longer I stayed, the more successful I became. That in turn made me more and more grateful. It was like being reborn, and I decided to break the chain of unhappiness that had been in my family past. All the crap has disappeared. I consider myself a first-generation Graham. My wife and I ingrained a completely different set of values in our two sons, and now I see them instilling those things in my grandchildren. It's just a wonderful feeling. The Kleenex again...just set the box over here.

I wasn't completely truthful about giving all my clubs away. I do keep one set of terrific irons at the house. A new driver, too, and the newest sand wedges, which are gorgeous and set up just beautifully. Hey, you never know.

Pete Dye

Pete Dye's wild, eclectic golf course designs changed modern architecture. He likes to say that all he wanted to do was force the golfer to think, but the smile working at the corners of his mouth also suggests he wanted to instill abject fear—and if you press, he'll admit as much. Dye threw island greens, railroad ties, mounds, and pot bunkers into his hole creations, and for good measure likes to position water on both sides of them. Tour players who were playing the TPC at Sawgrass for the first time had the sense they were playing golf while handcuffed with a revolver pointed at their head.

Dye is an interesting character because at heart he is a purist. His audacious designs run contrary to the head-on, idealistic air he presents. He talks in a chirpy, populist way, and it is not a put-on, but, again, that slight smile lets you know he relishes the role of the country rube who has put one over on the city folk. When he starts to get carried away with one criticism or another, his wife, Alice, who is listening from the other room, hollers "Pete!" and he checks himself. Dye turns out to be a deep, resonant person. He was a fine competitive amateur, as was Alice, and his work over several decades has brought him close to remarkable people across all generations and all walks of life. He is one of the game's great benefactors. His design fee for the course at Purdue University: one dollar.

○ ○ ○

A good designer makes sure the cartpath runs along the right-hand side of the women's tee. Ladies don't like showing their behinds to the rest of the foursome when they bend over to tee their ball.

It's easy to look out over a golf course and say, "I'm gonna make my lawn look like that." Just remember, the superintendent has all week to make his grass green. You only have Saturday morning.

Babe Zaharias was not only a great golfer, she was a tremendous Indian wrestler. She challenged me to a match in 1946, just after I got out of the parachute infantry. As we joined hands and stood toe to toe, I thought, "This will be easy." Ten seconds later, I was flat on my back.

I don't know whether spikeless shoes help greens or not. I play in sneakers.

I don't like wearing things on my hands. It's a good thing Alice never gave me a wedding band, because I would have lost it by now. I keep my wristwatch in my pocket.

About thirty years ago, I went with a friend to an Alcoholics Anonymous meeting, just to give him support. The stories they told described me exactly. I quit drinking then and there, and so did Alice. We haven't had a drink since.

People have the idea I'm in love with island greens. Well, I've designed two in fifty years. Once you're stereotyped, it's almost impossible to lose it.

I get a kick out of overtipping people who usually don't get any tip at all, like the girl at the ice-cream counter. It leaves her happy and makes my ice cream taste better.

Going out to the movies doesn't make a lot of sense to me. They all wind up on television anyway. Heck, a friend of ours took us to dinner with Robert Redford, and I didn't know he was an actor until we got in the car to go home.

No doubt about it, I'm a terrible dresser. Most old people are. The reason is, we know you won't form a lasting opinion of us based on the clothes we wear.

I don't own a car; I rent one year-round. You're looking at me like I'm crazy, but it's cheaper, believe me. I travel three hundred days a year, which means I'd have to rent a car most of the time anyway. So why invest $30,000 in one that sits in my driveway all year? I don't pay for parking at the airport. I can catch the first flight home to one of three airports—West Palm Beach, Miami, or Fort Lauderdale—because I live close to

all three and don't have to pick up that car I don't own. Plus, I earned enough points in the program to get Alice the use of one free for a year, so right now I have a two-for-one deal. I'm probably the only guy in America with car insurance who doesn't own a car. That policy was hard to get.

I wish Tiger Woods could be forced to hit his driver fourteen times a round. The distance he gets with his 2-iron is impressive, but the risk of a bad shot is cut in half. There's so little suspense to it.

Golf has changed, and so have the golfers. In 1960 the PGA Tour brought an event to the Indianapolis Speedway. It was played the same week as the Indianapolis 500. The final round was played through an unholy mess of chicken bones, beer cans, programs, and wrappers. The total purse was $50,000. As general chairman of the tournament, I remember sort of apologizing to Mike Souchak for the ruckus and bad playing conditions. His response was, "If you want to cut holes in the pavement, we'll play straight down Main Street for that kind of money."

I spent a night in jail when I was twelve. I got caught driving my dad's Model A Ford. My uncle was the town's mayor, and he thought a night in the slammer would make an impression on me. Did it ever. That was the last crime I ever committed.

I played in the U.S. Open at Inverness in 1957. The greens were mowed at a quarter-inch, compared with less than an eighth of an inch today. But that didn't mean they weren't fast. You could drop a ball on the back of one of the greens and it would ride the grain all the way to the front of the green. On the other hand, if you were putting uphill into the grain, you had to hammer the ball to hit it ten feet. Sidehill putts were very dicey. Grain was a wonderful component of green reading and judging how hard to hit the ball. I wish they would raise the mower heights a bit, so grain could be a factor again. At the very least, it would cut maintenance budgets in half so more people could afford to play.

I've worked on some pretty big projects, but never once have I used a contract. And I've gotten paid every time. All it takes is an ability to judge character.

Women tend to take golf more seriously than men. They play faster, dress better, follow the rules more closely. There are exceptions to every rule, but for the most part, I'm right.

If I've told the people at the rental-car counter once, I've told them a thousand times: I do not want the fuel option.

Gary McCord

One suspects that Gary McCord's zaniness as a TV announcer has to be 80 percent act and that when you meet with him face-to-face, a more restrained, sober-thinking individual will quickly reveal himself. It doesn't happen. Though McCord is a bit less animated, and he spews the calculated one-liners with some restraint, he basically is the same guy: a free-spirited Californian who sees golf from an oblique angle. He's quick to expose it as the inane, ridiculous, soul-scorching, psyche-ruining game that it is.

McCord's inclination to look for the humor and the bizarre in everything is admirable, for if ever there were a golfer driven to cynicism, it would be him. His career, though not quite a failure, had a shipwreck quality to it. He ground away on the PGA Tour for twenty-three years with nary a victory to show for it, and a pair of second-place finishes only intensified his frustration. That he emerged not only sane but whole is a tribute to his great sense of fun and humility.

o o o

Are you one of those forty-five-year-old amateurs who think they can make it on the Champions Tour? It takes cojones to think you're going to stare down Tom Watson in the final group on Sunday, and that's a good sign. But after you quit your day job and secure one of the seven spots available at Q school, you have exactly one year to get it done. You will play every single week and not come up for air, even if you pull a muscle in your toupee, because if you don't finish in the top thirty on the money list, you're done. Thanks for coming, and come back and see us soon. The bottom line is, it's the hardest tour to get on and stay on in the world.

The first time I played a PGA Tour event at Tucson was 1975. I came off the course on

Sunday feeling very good about myself. I'd finished at even par, and I knew I could play even better if I worked at it. I cleaned out my locker and stopped to watch the finish on TV. Johnny Miller, the leader, is playing the eighteenth hole at Tucson National, a long, hard par 4. Miller's got 225 yards uphill to a back-left pin and decides on a 4-wood. As soon as the ball leaves the clubface, Miller shouts, "Go in!" The ball bounces one foot behind the hole, and he makes it to shoot twenty-five under. I just stood there thinking, *Maybe I'm not good enough to be out here.* It was a long, sobering walk to the car, and a long twenty-four years on tour.

In Valdosta, Georgia, during a mini-tour event, a player named James Black bet me twenty dollars he could put five golf balls in his mouth and then close his mouth all the way. I tried it but could get only two in there. James put all five balls in, which was amazing, but then he said, "I'll give you a chance to get even. I bet I can fit a whole loaf of bread in my mouth." There's no way a human can do this! So I went out and got one of those extra-long loaves of Wonder Bread and took it back. James just smiled. He started compressing the bread—squeezed it, sat on it, stomped on it—and then began shoving it in his mouth. It took a while, but he got it all in there and closed his mouth. It was the damnedest thing I've ever seen, a bargain for the forty dollars it cost me.

Many years ago, in the throes of my struggles on the PGA Tour, I had difficulty even getting into pro-ams. I needed money, so I put together a forty-five-minute magic show I'd perform at corporate events surrounding the tournament. My interest in magic was kindled by Steve Martin, the comedian I'd gone to high school with. One time I even performed on TV during a rainout. My specialty is cards and coins. I'm not very good, but I talk so much nobody notices. Hey, I'm trying to be the total package.

People ask if I've ever had a bad day. One day in the early 1980s outside Flint, Michigan, I had just missed my fifth or sixth cut in a row by one shot. My first marriage had dissolved, I was dead broke, my game was terrible, and I had an unexplained rash. Standing in the locker room, I had a real stupid idea. I thought, I can punch the locker and break my hand. Collect the insurance and get my life back together. Here comes a hard right hand, over the top, but all I did was dent the locker. I hit it again, but still, nothing, except a bigger dent and some scraped knuckles. Two locker-room

attendants ran over and asked what was the matter. I sat there with my face in my hands, feeling like the guy in *It's a Wonderful Life,* who couldn't even kill himself properly. I looked up at the guys. "Fly was bothering me; I think I got it," I said. "Where's the tour next week?"

If you find yourself broke and essentially homeless, like I was coming out of my divorce, a concrete storage unit makes for suitable temporary housing. I rented a U-Lock-It and actually slept in it a few nights over roughly a two-week period. I was pleasantly surprised by how cheap, comfortable, and quiet it was. The amenities weren't much; I had to run an extension cord into the unit to power the night light and space heater. But plastic flowers improved the ambience.

I am the poster child for Attention Deficit Disorder. In the CBS broadcast booth I'm constantly thumbing through magazines while we're on the air. But golf is the perfect sport for someone with ADD. You only need to concentrate for a few minutes at a time, as Lee Trevino proved.

Where do I get my lines? Whatever's hot in pop culture, really. I jot little expressions into my laptop, and if something happens that fits, I'll use one. It's amazing the parallels you can construct between golf and celebrity boxing, the Osbournes, lip-syncing, or whatever. Most don't make the cut. Others do, for better or worse.

The "body bags" and "bikini wax" comments were merely the straw that broke the camel's back for me at the Masters. I don't think the Masters people were comfortable with my style from the beginning. One year a ball bounded over the fourteenth green and I remarked, "Oooh, that one's in the cheap seats." I silently began counting the seconds, and I didn't get to four before [producer] Frank Chirkinian shouted in my headpiece, "There are no cheap seats at Augusta National!" Eventually I found out he had a Batphone connection to [Augusta National's] Hord Hardin, who immediately let it be known this is not the type of thing we say at Augusta.

When I said about the seventeenth green, "They don't mow this green, they bikini wax it," I'd just read the phrase in a magazine. Moments earlier I was reading a story on the Golden Door spa near my home in Escondido, and it mentioned bikini waxes. Those words were on my mind, and they just popped out of my mouth. The president of CBS Sports, Neil Pilson, was sitting right next to me when I said it, and he laughed and the cameraman laughed. If someone laughs at Augusta, it's a bad sign. Chirkinian himself once told me, "If I laugh about something, it's not funny." Anyway, a short time later I was gone.

I never played in the Masters, of course. But I did get to play Augusta National during a practice round in the mid-1980s. I was with Mac O'Grady and Jodie Mudd, and when we came to the sixteenth hole, the flagstick was back left in its traditional Sunday location. Mac says, "Gary, let's not go for the hole; it's too easy. See that little shelf on the back right? It's very difficult to make the ball stay up there. It's probably the hardest shot on the course. Let's aim there." I said sure, and of course my ball doesn't stay on the shelf. It rolls sideways down the tier, all the way across the green and dives in the hole. The gallery, of course, goes wild. All the way to the green I'm bowing, waving, and smiling, saying quietly, "Thank you. . . .

I wasn't aiming there. . . . Thank you. . . . It was a terrible shot. . . . Thank you. . . . I stink."

I don't want to age the way Ben Hogan did. I met Hogan once, a story that has been well chronicled. But what stayed with me from that visit to Shady Oaks was when I went downstairs to the card room. A bunch of guys are playing gin, and they tell me they won't let Hogan in the card game because he's a little overbearing. Mr. Hogan, like a lot of old people who spend their lives being difficult, became lonely. Only then did he make an effort to be nicer to people, and I don't think it went down easy on him or others, because neither party was used to him being a people person. He was saying hello when it was time to say good-bye. I came away thinking, *I'm going to be nice my whole life.*

On the last hole at the Toshiba Classic in 1999, I needed to hole a long eagle putt to win my first tournament on either tour. I thought that was the deal until my good friend John Jacobs, who I'm paired with, holes his shot from thirty yards off the green. Now I need the putt to extend the playoff. The crowd is going crazy, and I'm playing along with the theatrics, making all sorts of gestures to make it fun and dramatic. It finally grows quiet and I settle in over the putt. Then it occurs to me: I haven't read the putt at all. I have no idea how it breaks, and I'm too embarrassed to step away. This is what age does to you. I decided to just hit the putt. Damned if it doesn't go in. I end up winning the playoff, and for a moment, getting old is a beautiful thing.

Before you move into the storage facility, get to know the security guard.

Kathy Whitworth

Unappreciated genius can be more awe-inspiring than talent we're accustomed to seeing. Kathy Whitworth is a case in point: Looking at her playing record is like discovering the Dead Sea scrolls. She won eighty-eight LPGA Tour tournaments, a record that has never been surpassed, including a hatful of majors. She guesses she finished second ninety-some times but shrugs it off: "Winning is all that mattered," she says. Whitworth has surprisingly little to show financially for one of the great athletic careers in women's sports history, and therein lies a small tragedy. At age sixty-seven, she is still working, partly to keep busy and in part because the money comes in handy.

Whitworth had more stories to tell than our magazine space could accommodate—another small tragedy. But though she didn't emerge rich or famous by Annika Sorenstam standards, her memories leave her beaming. And you can't put a price on that.

○ ○ ○

I started out trying to win one tournament. Then I wanted to win a second to prove the first one wasn't a fluke. Then I thought, *Maybe I can keep doing this.* The next thing I knew, I had eighty-eight.

The way Annika Sorenstam is going, she's got an awful good shot at breaking my record. Your next question is going to be, does that bother me? The answer is, not at all. I never thought about records when I was in the process of winning all those tournaments, anyway. For what it's worth, I don't think Annika loses sleep at night wondering if she'll win eighty-nine tournaments. She knows that record will be hers if she keeps doing what she's doing.

If not for a career decision by Mickey Wright, my total never would have set the record. Mickey was the best I've ever seen, without a doubt. She retired earlier than she had to, and if she'd kept going, she surely would have won more than the eighty-two she had when she quit for good. Just playing along normally, she easily could have won more than a hundred. I set a standard for Annika to surpass, but it would be a lot more interesting if Mickey hadn't hung up her spikes as soon as she did.

Here's how great Mickey was: Four years after her retirement in 1969, she decided to come back and play the Dinah Shore in 1973. That's a major championship, and with no tournaments in between, she teed it up and won. She retired again. Then, in 1979, she came back and played in the Coca-Cola Classic. And Nancy Lopez ran in a long putt to beat her and four others in a sudden-death playoff. Maybe it's the type of accomplishment only another pro athlete can appreciate, but let me tell you, that was strong stuff.

The press makes a big to-do about the number of top-ten finishes a player has. Like a lot of pros, I don't understand it. Mickey Wright finished second more than fifty times. My seconds numbered somewhere in the nineties. Gosh, I was in twenty-three sudden-death playoffs. Not one of those seconds felt very good. Each one was a testament to the fact that I hadn't played quite well enough to get the job done.

Many times I missed putts that would have won a tournament or gotten me into a playoff. Usually it was for the same reason: I was thinking about how badly I needed to make the putt instead of what I had to do to make it. Think about that. If you can get to a point where your routine, focus, and determination are so good that you truly treat every putt the same, you're going to be one tough player to beat.

I joined the LPGA Tour in 1959. At that time we played in a lot of small places: Caldwell, Idaho. Ogden, Utah. Las Cruces, New Mexico. Midland, Texas. The field was sometimes only thirty-five players. The bad news was that we paid only fifteen places or so. The good news was, there was no cut. The galleries were incredible; sometimes it seemed like the whole town was out there, and they got to walk along with us because there were no ropes. The enthusiasm was remarkable. Slowly, the small-market events on all three major tours are disappearing, and it's really a shame.

We helped each other. We shared cars, roomed together, and if someone was really struggling financially, we would help them get to the next town. A dollar went further, of course. Gas was fifteen cents a gallon, and a motel cost five dollars. We caravaned a lot, four or five cars, so we could be there for each other if there was a problem. There were no cell phones or even CB radios, so we communicated by holding up signs in the car windows—"I need to go to the bathroom" was flashed a lot. There was poor radio reception and no air conditioning, and I also got a lot of flat tires. So many, I got to where I could change a tire and be on my way in less than twenty minutes. Those experiences stay with you. Today, every time I get in my car I think how nice it is to have cruise control, air conditioning, and steel-belted radial tires.

In 1982 I was looking for a place to invest the money I had accumulated. I ended up investing a good piece of my worth in an equities firm. It was described as a sure-win thing, but a couple of years later, there were rumors it was having problems. I was assured by everyone that things were going just fine. Well, this company went out of business almost overnight, and a lot of people were wiped out. Athletes, doctors, professional people—a lot of lives were ruined, and there were a number of suicides. Me, I lost virtually all of my retirement.

I had to go back to work, and that meant going back on tour. That was a very difficult time in my life, because I'd never played golf feeling like I had to do it to survive. The fun was gone, and I didn't play worth a darn. But I had no choice but to keep playing, because it was an inroad to pro-ams and outings, anything I could do to get back on my feet. No job was too small, and I worked a lot harder than I wanted to.

I came out of it eventually. It was a gut-wrenching time, but I'm very proud to have worked my way out of it.

There is concern about the number of foreign players dominating on the LPGA Tour. The top Americans aren't even in the major-ity anymore, but that sits fine with me. Remember, we're getting the very best these countries have to offer. And a great many of them—Annika for instance—learned to play over here. When people ask why we aren't developing more top players, I say, "We are. Look at Annika."

My mother was a huge collector of S&H Green Stamps. Remember those? They were given out as a premium for buying gas, groceries, and whatnot. When you filled a certain number of books with stamps you'd trade them in for merchandise. To my mother these green stamps were like gold. One day she gave me some of her books to buy a Spalding driver and 3-wood. Real clubs, and new! I felt so privileged. Many years later, I won a tournament called the S&H Green Stamp Classic. First-prize money was modest, but the sponsor threw in a ton of those books already filled with stamps. My mother was at the awards presentation, and when they gave me all those books, the longing in my mother's eyes was too much for me. I gave her all of those stamps, and it was like I'd just handed her a winning lottery ticket. It's one of my happiest memories.

The little course I started out on had nine holes. The third hole was a par 4 that came back toward the clubhouse. The green was right by the first tee, and if we didn't like our score after three holes, we'd call it a warmup and just start over. Sometimes we started over four times. There was many a round in my career when I wished I could do that.

I never could wear a hat or even a visor. They gave me a headache, for one thing. I wore my hair too high, for another. There are hat people, and I'm not one of them. Not that it did my skin any good.

If a player wants to exploit their attractiveness, that's fine. I had no objection to Jan Stephenson taking advantage of the beauty God gave her and have no problem at all with any individual who chooses to do that. I would dislike it if the LPGA Tour pro-moted its players' looks instead of their golf. The reason is, it hurts the product in the long run. Again using Jan as an example, she was one of the best players of her era, a very hard worker and fine competitor. But today I believe she's remembered more for posing for a calendar. I might be different, but even if I were gorgeous, as a pro golfer I'd like to be remembered more for what I achieved with my clubs.

I started seeing Harvey Penick in 1957, before I turned pro. My mother and I drove from New Mexico to Austin for three days of lessons. We spent most of the first day in Harvey's office, getting to know each other, which he thought was important. Then we went to hit balls. After I hit for quite a while, Harvey sat me down again and said, "I think I can help you. But you'll have to do exactly what I tell you to do. If you don't follow the advice I want to give you, I'm afraid it will be a waste of your time and my time. Are you willing to do that?" I told him I would do exactly as he said, and he smiled and said, "I think we'll do very well together." Harvey turned out to be my only teacher for twenty-five years.

Harvey put a lot of emphasis not just on what he said but how he said it. He was very careful about phrasing things in a way that wouldn't hurt your confidence or cause you to misunderstand him. He started by modifying my grip, which he thought was the foundation for everything. He emphasized placing my hands on the club as opposed to twisting them into place. He told me to practice placing my hands on the grip, and that's pretty much all I did from eight a.m. to five p.m. He told me to do it at home until it became second nature. He said two things that really stuck with me. One was, "If you have a good grip, it will be easier to make a good swing than a bad one." The other was, "If you have a bad grip, you don't want a good swing." After I got the grip down pat, I started getting real good, real fast.

It's well known that Harvey's fee was very modest and that sometimes he didn't charge a student at all. Someone once suggested to Harvey that he increase his rate. Harvey said, "I guess I could charge more, but then I'd have to tell them more, and I don't think I could teach as well that way." Harvey was pure gold, through and through.

Harvey understood human nature. He'd tell me something and say, "I'm going to leave you now, and I want you to think about what I told you. Don't just stand out here and hit balls." Harvey would disappear but would secretly keep an eye on me. Of course, I'd digress into just mindlessly hitting balls, and then he would come back. He'd tell a small story unrelated to the lesson, then he'd quickly say, "Let's see you hit a good shot." Of course, I couldn't do it because I'd stopped thinking about what he'd told me before he walked away the first time. I felt embarrassed and sort of ashamed. But Harvey said gently, "Kathy, you must remember to keep your mind on the thing you're working on." Then he disappeared again, his point drilled into me as clearly as though he'd screamed it. From then on I became a very productive practicer.

One time I fell into a terrible slump, and I worked for months trying to play myself out of it. Finally I went to see Harvey. It took him two full days to diagnose the problem and find a solution. After he had detected the flaw, explained it, and told me what to do to fix it, I was cured almost immediately. But as I left, he said, "Kathy, don't you ever let it get this bad again before you come see me." He said that because he didn't like to see me struggling, but also because the elusiveness of the solution frightened him. I was touched by that.

If you want to get to know someone, make a long trip by car with them.

Arnold Palmer

Arnold says he is a morning person, and when he comes into his office at Bay Hill at nine sharp, he says he has been up for four hours already. He looks it. His eyes are clear, his complexion is sound, and he moves quickly. Oddly, he looks his best when he is not doing the thing he was born to do, which is play golf. He is a great host and a fine interview, cheerful, funny, not too cautious. He treats me to mild profanity thirty minutes into the interview, and sixty minutes in, a stronger one. I'm earning his trust, and that is the frustrating part—it is impossible to cover all that he is about in a short visit. But Arnold does his best, and in the end the best parts of him come through.

○ ○ ○

My whole career, I never missed a tee time. Not once, which I suppose is saying a lot for a career that's spanned sixty years and thousands of rounds of golf. Now, for many years I've had a recurring dream that I miss my tee time. In the dream there's no consequence because I wake up abruptly. You can't imagine the relief, realizing that it was just a dream. Now that I'm retired, I'm hoping to hell that dream will go away.

It interests me how Phil Mickelson is perceived as being too aggressive. It interests me because Tiger is every bit as aggressive as Phil. Look at some of the shots Tiger hits into the green from the wrong fairway, the long shots over water, the tremendous shots he hits from the trees. There's been one difference between the two guys, and it's that Tiger is in good enough shape physically to pull them off. I'm serious. If Phil were in

better condition, he'd have a lot more success when he goes for broke. He probably has as much raw talent as Tiger, but his body might rob him of a little precision in those situations where he really needs it.

I get invited to weddings of the sons and daughters of friends of mine, and I always end up crying. Sometimes I haven't even met the young people. When I watch the movie *Northwest Passage* with Spencer Tracy, I cry. Not because it's that kind of movie, but because Tracy's character reminds me of my father. So, yes, I'd say I'm a sentimental guy.

Toward the end, I was playing tournaments on the Champions Tour because the tournaments and their sponsors asked me to play. The last couple of years, it wasn't easy to do that. I'm a proud man, and to play like I did

was embarrassing, and downright painful. Just terrible for me. Playing in the Father-Son with my grandson Sam, I could sort of hide because Sam's a good player. I enjoyed that. But the official events, it got to a point where whatever good I was doing for the tournament didn't compensate for the emotional pain it put me through.

If you have a child just starting out in the game, one of the best things you can do is get him a push mower—a lawn mower with no engine. When I was a kid, one of my responsibilities was to mow the lawn with the type of push mower everybody used in those days. Between that and driving a tractor that didn't have power steering, I got strength in my hands and forearms that never really went away, and which helped me enormously in golf. Push mowers are hard to find, but getting one will do your junior golfer more good than just about any swing trainer.

I sure wish the decorum around our game was better. If we just dressed a little neater, I'd be happy. There's a trend in some circles to not care at all—wear your hat backward, don't tuck your shirt in, don't iron anything. That isn't style, it's just not caring.

My shirttail hung out a lot. But heck, I had a thin waist and the kind of swing that tended to untuck my shirt for me. But I started out with it tucked in—that's the difference.

I've got hundreds of persimmon drivers. Years ago I could always go and choose one if the one I was using wasn't working. Then metal woods came along, and overnight I went from owning hundreds of backup drivers to owning a museum. It's sad that these great works of art have no practical use anymore.

I was scared to lose. Just terrified of it. The first part of my career especially, the fear of doing my best and it not being good enough, of failing, was a huge motivating force for me. Jackie Burke says many great champions are basically insecure people who are secretly afraid of returning to the background they came out of, and that might have been true with me.

We all love winning, but losing carried some connotations that just made it unacceptable to me. I was a gracious loser, but I sure did hate getting beat.

You can't be scared standing on the first tee. You've got to learn to deal with that. I had a system. I made my mind go back to the most basic fundamentals of the game: my grip, my stance, the position of my head, the very first things I learned. It became a habit. If you watch old videos of me getting ready to play, you'll see me gripping and regripping the club, waggling, taking my stance, and then standing normally. I'm reviewing the fundamentals. It made me think of what I should be doing, as opposed to how important it was. I highly recommend it.

There were times when I stood on the eighteenth tee feeling my life would all but end if I didn't win, and when I didn't win, I discovered my life in fact did not end. When I lost to Billy Casper at Olympic [in the 1966 U.S. Open], I found afterward that in many ways my life improved. In the aftermath of that loss and a few others, more of life came calling, and I continued on with a slightly different perspective. I was better for the experience. In a roundabout way, I'm telling you why Tiger breaking Jack's record is not a gimme. I realize Tiger has only seven majors to go, but the truth is, we don't know what his desires might be a year or two, or five, from now. Never assume you know those things.

Ever stand over a putt and just know you were going to make it? That great feeling where the putt's as good as in, that all you have to do is stroke it? Hundreds of golfers have described the sensation to me, and I still don't know what they're talking about. In my day I was a good putter, and there were times when my confidence ran high, but I never felt that premonition. I was so desperate to make every putt that I focused very hard and didn't take any chances. When I birdied seventeen and eighteen to win the Masters in 1960—I made a long putt on seventeen—I guess I was in a frame of mind to make the putts. But I never felt I was in a zone where it seemed like the golf gods were giving me putts. I felt like I earned every one of them.

I'll always argue that the worst thing you can do is leave a putt short. I'll never understand any of the arguments to the contrary, because they're basically saying that you should stand over the putt hoping not to three-putt. Get the ball to the hole no matter what. If you get the ball to the hole, you at least give it a chance to go in. Which, if I'm not mistaken, is the object of the game.

Bad weather was a huge problem for my generation. The raingear was terrible; none of it was really waterproof. There were no nonslip gloves, and the grips all got slippery. The golf courses had very poor drainage systems. Courses would mow the fairways as close as they dared because the tour was in town, and there often wasn't that much grass to begin with. So when it rained, the fairways turned into mud. The

mud would cake on our leather shoes something terrible; you'd scrape it off, take two steps, and it would be right back on there. You gave up. In the 1950s, many a time I was five-eleven when I teed off and six-one when I walked off. When our leather shoes got wet, they weighed a couple of pounds apiece.

You ever watch those NFL games played in the 1950s, the crappy helmets and pads and big, heavy cleats they wore? What we had was the golf equivalent of that.

It's pretty well known that Ben Hogan didn't bond with anyone, but I have to say, he was particularly chilly to me. He very pointedly referred to me as "Fellah," even face-to-face. I just accepted it, and in the end he wasn't my type of guy anyway. I wasn't a special case; he didn't bond with Nelson or Snead, either. He was cordial to them but never was close to either man. He never grew close to any golfer, with the possible exceptions of Jackie Burke and Jimmy Demaret. For all of the talk of my rivalry with Jack Nicklaus, at heart we truly like each other. I can't say the same for Ben Hogan and me.

If you hit a darned good drive but it takes a bad kick and goes out of bounds by a foot, it's two strokes. Period. If you fan it—miss the ball completely—it's one stroke. I've never understood that.

Of all the tournaments that got away—and I let a lot get away—the one that hurt the most was the 1961 Masters. I made the most terrible mistake a golfer can make, which is taking it for granted I was going to win. I double-bogeyed the last hole to lose by one to Gary Player, and it hurt so much—and still does—that I never let it happen again. Losing to Casper at Olympic, coming up short in the Open playoff against Jack at Oakmont in '62, none of them was nearly as painful as Augusta in '61.

One of the great mysteries in golf is how you can be playing great and then suddenly lose your game in the middle of a round. It happened to me at Olympic. When the train leaves the tracks, it's very rare you can get it back on track. I think what happens is, you get a little anxious. That causes you to start swinging quickly, and worse, thinking quickly. You start pressing, for distance mainly but sometimes trying to pull off shots you have no business trying. It's very hard—impossible, really—to reverse your thinking and go back to the frame of mind you were in just a couple of holes before. It happens to even the finest players, and when it happens, they could have the best sport psychologist in the world caddieing for them and he couldn't help.

Of all the people I've met, one man stands a little above the rest: Dwight Eisenhower had a presence about him that was just profound. On the occasions I was with him, he exuded a type of character I hadn't experienced before and haven't quite experienced since. He was humble and sincere, yet also honest and direct. Ike is the only person I've met who made me feel a little starstruck.

I was scheduled to play golf with President John Kennedy, but it was canceled. Jimmy Carter didn't play golf, and I'm not sure Lyndon Johnson did, either. I played horseshoes with George W. Bush up in Kennebunkport, but not golf. So I played golf with only six presidents: Eisenhower, Nixon, Ford, Reagan, the first President Bush, and Bill Clinton. That's pretty good. You know somebody who's played with more?

Acknowledgments

I am indebted to the team of people who brought these interviews to print. Collecting the words was not the half of it.

I should acknowledge first the photographers who charmed our subjects into these intriguing portraits, beginning with Ben Van Hook, who captured Sam Snead as no shooter had. Other photographers who did their best work for the series are Joey Terrill, Darren Carroll, J.D. Cuban, Joe McNally, Dom Furore, Eric Larson, and Peter Gregoire, led by our incandescent photo editor, Matt Ginella.

Mike O'Malley, the heroic *Golf Digest* executive editor, curry-combed the passages, smoothed them out, and placed them in logical order. It's amazing what a comma here, a semicolon there, and a judicious eye everywhere can do to a passage, and O'Malley is the rare editor who can parse out sentences while applying his gifted ear.

The franchise was his from the get-go, and he was devoted to it. We once had an argument whether the secondary photos should be accompanied by captions. I disliked them, he felt they were necessary. His reasoning wore me down, and it occurred to me as a I hung up the phone that he cared about *My Shot* at least as much as I did. A talented editor with a strong back and soft touch—a writer can't ask for more than that. Mike also helped me choose interviews that merited inclusion here.

Sue Ellen Powell, our chief of research, was charged with fact-checking every item in every installment.

Ultimately it was the voices of the subjects and their willingness to reveal themselves, though, that made the series and, I hope, this book special.

I thank them all.